ORGANIZE
— YOUR —
FAMILY!

Other books in the series

Organize Your Home!
Organize Your Office!

ORGANIZE
YOUR
FAMILY!

**Simple Routines
That Work for You
and Your Kids**

Ronni Eisenberg
with Kate Kelly

NEW YORK

Copyright © 1993 Ronni Eisenberg with Kate Kelly

Library of Congress Cataloging-in-Publication Data

Eisenberg, Ronni.
Organize your family! : simple routines that work for you and your kids / by Ronni Eisenberg with Kate Kelly.
p.   cm.
ISBN 1-56282-871-1
1. Home economics.   2. Parents—Time management.   3. Children—Time management.   4. Parenting.   I. Kelly, Kate, 1950-
II. Title.
TX147.E46   1993
640—dc20   92-43632
CIP

Text design by Carla Weise/Levavi & Levavi

First Edition
10 9 8 7 6 5 4 3 2 1

This book is dedicated
with love, humor, and affection
to the children in our lives:

Mandi
Elizabeth
Julia
Caroline
Harrison
Joy

Contents

Introduction

Since my profession is teaching how to be better organized, people often explain to me why they *aren't* organized. One of the more frequent reasons I hear is: "I have children."

That's why I've written *Organize Your Family!* I know how difficult it is to get through a stack of mail or even the newspaper when you've got children who are continually thinking of other things for you to do. Your responsibilities start with feedings and diaper changes and increase to reading stories, chauffeuring, producing birthday parties, and cheering at Little League games, not to mention cleaning up spilled apple juice, labeling an entire wardrobe for camp, and endlessly picking up and putting away.

Having children makes it more important than ever to get organized. Now you not only have to get yourself out of the house in the morning with all the things you need, but you're also responsible for getting one, two, three, or more children out of the house with everything *they* need. And that's just the morning . . . Your evening hours will likely be spent overseeing homework, schedules, chores, and bedtime while still having to keep the household on an even keel.

All parents want less stress and more time for enjoying family life (and for stealing a few moments for themselves!), and that's what *Organize Your Family!* promises to do—make your life easier. I've taken basic organizing principles and applied them to situations that affect the family. What's more, every suggestion has been through a "reality" check. Between us, my coauthor and I have six children, who have (whether they meant to or not) tested all the advice contained in this book.

Because I know you're short on time, the book is written in such a way that you can spend five minutes referring to a single topic or a few hours scanning the entire book for lots of ideas. So dive into *Organize Your Family!* If you implement even a fraction of the suggestions here, I promise you a less chaotic, more manageable world.

ORGANIZE
YOUR
FAMILY!

1

BIRTHDAY PARTIES:
Party Planning
Made Easy

Party-Giving Basics

Birthday Party Countdown

The ingredients for a good birthday party are timeless. What I draw upon for a party for my children are the same trimmings my mother needed for a party for me: a fun theme, lively decorations, special friends, food, favors, and games, all capped off with a rousing chorus of "Happy Birthday."

Though these elements are not complex, pulling off a successful party while keeping up with our busy lives is no simple feat. Here's a guide to doing it well—and smoothly:

PARTY-GIVING BASICS

The family should agree on general party elements:

• *Type of party.* What does your child want, and what can you manage? There are three basic choices:

1. At-home party with family-run activities.
2. At-home party with hired entertainer (singer? magician?).
3. Party away from home—gymnastics or bowling party; visit to the zoo or children's museum; movie, etc.

• *Length of party.* Stay within these guidelines:

TODDLERS	AGES 3–5	SCHOOL AGE
1–1 hr. 15 min.; with parents	90 minutes; some parents still staying	2 hours

• *Number of guests.* A rule of thumb is to invite one more than the age of the child: A youngster turning three would have four guests. When these numbers don't work and you need to throw a bigger bash, ask parents to stay or request extra help from friends or relatives so that there will be plenty of hands to help the children have fun.

• *Food.* Plan a simple child-oriented menu. (Avoid obvious trouble—chocolate and grape juice stain.) Remember, too, that decorating cupcakes, assembling English muffin pizzas, or making sundaes can be great party activities. If parents are going to stay, put out a coffee urn and crackers and cheese or a coffee cake.

• *Activities and entertainment.*

For toddlers.   Plan familiar activities such as painting, working with clay, or playing in the backyard. A group activity such as singing will involve them for ten to fifteen minutes.

Ages three to five. Offer simple craft projects, and play games like Duck, Duck Goose, Simon Says, and Mother May I?

School age. Try treasure hunts, relay races, acting out

short scenes, and more complex crafts such as painting a T-shirt.

Preteens. Outings to a movie, an ice rink, or a sports-activities center are generally popular for this age group.

• *Facilities.* For an at-home party, plan the use of the house, and deem certain rooms "off-limits" (e.g., the living room and bedrooms). For a party held elsewhere, consider convenience—can guests get there easily? Will you be able to supervise adequately? (A spot that would be terrific for nine-year-olds might be a nightmare with a younger group.)

SMART TIP!

• *Favors.* Favors should be the same for all guests. If the girls are receiving "pearl" necklaces, then the boys will need something different, but don't personalize more than that. (If boy- and girl-favors are different, use two colors of bags.) As party bags, try using plastic buckets, brown bags decorated with paint or stickers, or plastic bags stuffed with colored tissue paper and tied with coordinated ribbon.

• *Gifts.* At a party for preschoolers, gifts should be tucked away and opened after the party. (Children this age sometimes have difficulty with the concept of "giving" and "ownership.") By school-age, gift-opening can become an enjoyable part of a traditional party.

BIRTHDAY PARTY COUNTDOWN

Two Months in Advance

• Discuss with your child his or her party wishes and start investigating. Visit the bowling alley, or investigate magicians, and check recommendations.

• Select the exact date and time of your party, based on family convenience and the availability of the facilities and/or entertainer. Don't forget to cross-check the date against school holidays and vacation time. Book necessary arrangements, and put it on the family calendar.

Four-Six Weeks in Advance

• Firm up the guest list and create a Master List. This information will be useful from the time you address the first invitation until the last thank-you note is mailed.

WORTH THE TIME!

GUEST'S NAME AND ADDRESS	COMING? YES OR NO	GIFT	THANKS SENT

• Start purchasing decorations, candles, plates, cups, napkins, plastic utensils, tablecloths, moist towelettes (for sticky fingers), favors.
• Firm up decision on menu.
• Organize the details of the party and write a schedule, complete with specific activities. In general, parties follow this plan:

1. Flexible activity to keep guests busy during arrival.
2. Main activity of the party.
3. Cake (possibly preceded by a meal).
4. Wind down with quiet activity or gift-opening.

- Plan more activities than you think you'll need. That way, if a game flops or something takes less time than you expected, you've still got something for the kids to do.

- If you are doing the party yourself, establish a shoe box or paper bag for all the supplies needed for each game. Repack the supplies carefully after any test runs.

- On the schedule also note items such as what time the ice cream cake should be removed from the freezer. (Almost every family has had *one* party where the cake was still hard as a rock when the kids were all gathered at the table!)

- Plan for the unexpected:

IMPORTANT! —What if it rains and you intended the party to be outdoors? (Set a rain date or have an indoor plan.)

—What if someone is injured at a roller-skating party? (Have an extra adult there assigned to "emergencies.")

- Decide whether a sibling will be permitted to invite a friend.

- Assess what help you'll need, and ask relatives and/ or friends if you can count on them. Helpers can fill several roles; tell them what they are:

—Greeter: Usually the birthday child
—Gift-taker: Particularly important if the gifts are to be tucked away for later
—Get-the-guests-settled helper: After the guests have been greeted, someone should usher them in and help them join in the activity
—Game director
—Photographer
—Food-server (all food should be prepared in advance)
—Safety supervisor (for outdoor party)

—Party-bag distributor

—Secretary: Notes on the Master List what gift was from whom

—Troubleshooter: Available to take kids to the bathroom, soothe the child who falls, comfort the one who realizes his mother left . . .

Three Weeks in Advance

• Address and mail invitations. Request an "RSVP."

• Include a map if your home or the place where the party is to be held is difficult to find.

Ten Days Before

• Prepare party bags.

• Confirm entertainer and/or your reservation at a specific party locale.

• Order balloons and cake (or buy ingredients).

• Is your child expected to bring cupcakes to school to celebrate there? Make in advance and freeze.

One Week Before

• Confirm the cake and balloons.

• Are you borrowing chairs or tables from friends? Call and set a time when you can pick them up.

The Day Before

SMART TIP!   • Do as much decorating in advance as possible. Streamers can be hung, any theme-party decorating can be done, and the table can be set. (Instead of a tablecloth, try putting butcher

---

WHEN THE PARTY IS HELD AWAY FROM HOME

- Pack a large shopping bag with:

    —cake knife
    —candles and matches
    —plates
    —cups
    —napkins
    —plastic utensils
    —tablecloths and any necessary decorations
    —juice or soda
    —garbage or shopping bags for bringing gifts home
    —moist towelettes
    —camera

- Load a second shopping bag with all the prepacked favors.

---

paper on the table, and set out crayons. The guests can decorate the "cloth" while waiting for their food.)

Day of Party

- Prepare food early in the day.
- Have premoistened towelettes or baby wipes on hand in the room where food will be served and in any location where the kids' hands could get messy.
- Discuss with your child the party schedule and any awkward situations:

    —If the gifts will be opened at the party, talk about what to say if your child already has the gift or doesn't like it.

—Who sits next to the party person? Try putting the birthday child at the head of the table, and then conduct an orderly game of musical chairs for the guests. When the music stops, that's where they stay.

• Put your pets in a safe place.

Writing Thank-Yous

• Supply your child with his or her own stationery, or provide cards or paper to decorate with stickers beforehand.

TIME SAVER! • Using the Master List, preaddress all the envelopes.

• Ask your child to write two or three notes per day. The preschooler can draw a "thank you" picture; ages five to seven may be able to do a short note, particularly if you create a form letter that can be copied: Dear ———, Thank you for the ——— and for coming to my party. Love, ———. Have your child check off names on the Master List as the notes are written.

ORGANIZATION PLUS! • Some parents purchase stickers to send along as an extra party "favor" with the note; a few superorganized families have taken pictures at the birthday party and enclose a snapshot of the party guest along with the thank-you. These touches aren't necessary, but they provide a terrific ending for a special event!

2

BIRTHDAY PARTIES:
Gift-Giving for Kids

WHAT'S AHEAD

Establishing a Gift Center

Stocking Up on Gifts

Including Your Child in the Process

Children love receiving birthday invitations, but a newly arrived invitation is often met with a parental groan: "Not another gift to shop for!" To avoid a last-minute shopping trip and to keep a step or two ahead of this rite of celebration, read on.

ESTABLISHING A GIFT CENTER

• Establish a closet shelf or several drawers as a gift center where you can store wrapping materials as well as gifts purchased in advance. If you're really tight on space, try an underbed storage unit.

```
┌─────────── SUPPLIES TO HAVE ON HAND ───────────┐
```

For wrapping:

- —wrapping paper, primarily birthday paper, but pick up some all-occasion and plain tissue paper as well
- —gift bags. These gaily-colored "shopping" bags come in a variety of sizes and make wrapping easy.
- —gift tags
- —ribbon
- —scissors
- —tape and dispenser ⎫ to be left in gift center
- —nonsmear pen ⎭
- —storage box in which to collect the above

For card-making:

- —blank note cards—postcard-weight stock (large stationery stores sell them in colors with matching envelopes)
- —colored markers and crayons
- —special stickers that your kids like
- —small box or zip-lock bag to store card-making supplies

STOCKING UP ON GIFTS

TIME AND MONEY SAVER! • When you find an age-appropriate gift (particularly if it's a bargain), buy a half-dozen and put them away, or choose an all-purpose gift and buy in bulk (ask for a discount).

• If a store provides gift-wrapping, and you don't have to wait in another line for it, let the store wrap the gifts.

If you're buying several presents, ask the clerk to identify them with a removable label.

• If your child receives duplicates of an item and you can't exchange it, add one of the toys to your own "gifts to give" shelf. (With a removable label, note who gave you the gift so you don't pass it back to them!)

• Store these gifts near your wrapping supplies—don't tuck them all over the house or you'll never find them again!

INCLUDING YOUR CHILD IN THE PROCESS

• To include your child in the planning, take school-age children to the store with you, or give them a catalog to scan. They can help you select the items to have on hand for upcoming parties.

• From toddlerhood on, your child can participate by making the card. Using the card-making supplies listed above, your child can have fun making an attractive card to attach to the gift. For the five-to-seven-year-old crowd, include in the supplies an index card showing the correct spelling of "Happy Birthday" so that you needn't spell it out each time.

SMART TIP!   • Let your little ones contribute wrapping paper. Most nursery schools use oversized paper for the children's paintings, and you can use their artwork to wrap a gift. It's a great way to recycle what you can no longer hang in the kitchen, and children feel proud of their artistic contributions.

3

CARPOOLING:
Organizing a Car (or Transportation) Pool

As your children get older, setting up transportation pools to school and to extracurricular activities can save time and be essential to your mental health by cutting down on the mind-numbing hours spent going to and from various places. Even city residents can "car pool," using buses and taxis to and from school, extracurricular classes, and birthday parties.

SETTING UP A CAR POOL

When it comes to ferrying children back and forth, there are only a few basic variations:

1. One parent takes "to," the other takes "from." Duties are rotated as families see fit.

2. One family takes responsibility for getting the children to *and* from their destination. For some school car pools, one family will transport both ways for a whole week; then it's the next family's turn. This method also makes sense if you're driving some distance to a class or using public transportation where so much time is invested in the initial travel.

• Once you have a basic plan, assign specific responsibilities at least a month in advance.

TIME SAVER!   • Save time by adding families. Establish a method, and share the carpooling evenly.

• Adjust the system as needed. In one three-family car pool, one mother could only do the "to" driving. She never picked up and, therefore, never was delayed by the teacher who frequently dismissed the class late. To compensate, she volunteered to drive one extra turn each month.

• Don't rule out carpooling with a family where both

WHAT TO AVOID IN A CAR POOL

- **Lateness.** Families who are chronically late will drive a prompt family mad.
- **Discord.** If you team up with a family whose children and yours dislike each other, fighting and hurt feelings may be the result.
- **Being taken.** Some people are artful at dodging responsibility just as it's their turn. If you have already seen a parent exhibit this quality, don't ask for trouble by agreeing to car pool with them.

parents work. Some families agree to do all the driving to weekday tennis lessons if the working-couple family drives to weekend activities. Think of other creative ways to repay uneven carpooling. Perhaps the family who drives less can run errands for the other family.

CARPOOLING ISSUES TO DISCUSS IN ADVANCE

• Check your insurance coverage regarding transporting others. You may need to add extra medical coverage for nonfamily-member passengers. If your babysitter will be driving your car, she can be covered as well, but discuss this with your insurance agent. If she's using her own car, she should double-check her car insurance coverage, and you should ask to see a copy of her policy.

• All participants should agree on "designated" drivers. Is everyone in the group comfortable with having your sitter or a willing relative take charge on a day when you can't do it?

• What if your child is sick? Some members of school car pools expect a family to drive on their day whether or not their child goes to school. If someone absolutely can't do it, they are responsible for finding the substitute and returning the favor.

KEEPING TRACK

• Each participating family should be given a carpooling chart such as the following:

CARY'S CAR POOL--May

	Mon.	Tues.	Wed.	Thurs.	Fri.
AM	Smith	Miller	Linden	White	Smith
PM	Linden	White	Smith	Miller	Linden

Mary and Joe Smith 555-2111   **Susan and Herb Miller 555-0021**
Janet and Bob Linden 555-9308   **Cathy and Ron White 555-4511**

ORGANIZATION PLUS! • Take your copy of the chart and enter on the family calendar all the times you drive. Also write down which parents are responsible for other days so that you can tell at a glance whom to call if arrangements for a particular day need to be changed. Save the original chart in an appropriate file.

• Try to establish a system and stick to it so that you aren't constantly phoning to rearrange the car pool.

ITEMS TO HAVE ALONG

• Pack the following in a small tote:
  —tissues
  —moist towelettes
  —emergency snacks and/or juice boxes
  —plastic bag for disposables
  —carry a few toys if a baby or toddler is along for the carpool ride; a magazine for yourself if you're carpooling alone

ALTERNATIVES TO CARPOOLING

There may come a time when you feel you just can't drive one more child one more place. There are alternatives:

• Can your children walk or bike on their own?

TIME SAVER! • Look for teachers who come to the house.

• Do you need to trim your children's schedules? Perhaps they are participating in too many activities. Cut back, or encourage them to take advantage of programs at school or in the neighborhood.

• Consider hiring a driver. A college student or retiree might be eager for a little part-time work. Inquire about their driving records, ask about any medications they might be taking, and ask for references. Check these carefully. Also call your insurance agent. Some states require you to carry workers' compensation coverage for this type of employee. If an automobile accident should occur, you'll want to be covered.

4

CHILD CARE:
Teaching a New Nanny or Housekeeper Your Household Routine

A person's style for training household help can run the gamut from being pushy and overbearing to "Here are the kids, you're on your own . . ." To have a well-run home, you have to be there to provide thorough, thoughtful, and specific training in the beginning. The long-term payoff will be a home that is managed the way you want it to be.

STEP ONE: GENERAL INTRODUCTIONS

IMPORTANT! • Plan to be at home for the first day, and easily available the first week so that the employee can observe your routine with the children.

• Asking your previous caregiver to train the new person can work—and save you time—*if* you've been pleased with her and she's leaving without bitterness.

• Clarify by what name you would like to be addressed.

• Security measures and emergency procedures should be introduced early on the first day. Demonstrate how the telephone works, where your emergency telephone list is, and where you leave other emergency instructions. Emphasize what security measures you take when answering the door.

• Let your children give a tour of the house. You can go along to point out items like the baby's intercom, how the back door locks, or why you keep a certain door closed.

STEP TWO: REVIEWING THE JOB AND ESTABLISHING COMMUNICATION

• When you hire your employee you should discuss job specifics: arrival time, departure time, paid holidays, vacation given, when you need to be alerted in case of employee illness, what provisions she's made if she has children and they get sick, and what attire you expect to be worn on the job. All these items should be reviewed at this time.

• Set a daily time for comparing notes on the day.

• Speak up promptly if something bothers you. On-the-spot feedback will help her do a better job.

STEP THREE: INTRODUCING THE CHILDREN'S ROUTINE

WORTH THE TIME! • Use a giant wall calendar to introduce the daily routine (see Chapter 7). Each morning review it together. Prepare a list of any household occurrences (plumber? furniture delivery?) for that day.

GETTING YOUR CAREGIVER FROM HERE TO THERE

- Provide your nanny or sitter with a street map and subway and bus guide, and review them with her.

TIME SAVER! • Create a "Directions" file. (For easy retrieval, directions should be filed alphabetically by person or place.)

- Write directions neatly (even if it means recopying them) on a large (4" × 6") index card. (It's a good size for carrying in a purse or tote, and it won't bend or tear the way paper will.) On each card, note the destination, the phone number of the place to which they are traveling, and *your* phone number in case she needs to call you. After it's used, the card should be filed and saved for the next time.
- Directions should be as specific as possible, noting landmarks as well as street names. Directions for public transportation in the city should specify bus stops. Clarify what the fare is and whether she'll need a bus transfer.
- Give instructions on tipping taxi drivers.
- Tell your caregiver the family travel rules regarding seat belts, snacks, etc.
- Provide her with a few extra dollars in case of emergency.

• You may also want to provide your helper with a list of activities that you would like her to do with your child—go for a walk, read, work puzzles, or paint.

• During the first week, talk about child-related issues: bathtime, bedtime, discipline, manners, safety, toilet training.

• Discuss your child's personality and any behavior characteristics that need watching: Your toddler loves scaling bookcases, or your five-year-old needs ten minutes to ease into a new situation. Offer helpful suggestions.

• Family rules should be written down or reviewed:

—Children should wash hands before eating.
—Eating permitted only at meals and snack time.
—Limit television time to one hour per day.

SMART TIP! • After any discussion, always ask, "Do you have questions?"

STEP FOUR: INTRODUCING THE HOUSEHOLD RESPONSIBILITIES

• Discuss with your new employee:

—How to answer the telephone; where to leave messages.
—How you create a shopping list (ask her to write items down when you are low, not out).
—How groceries should be put away.

ORGANIZATION PLUS! • Show the nanny or housekeeper each appliance (dishwasher, washer, dryer, vacuum) she will be using, and demonstrate how it operates. Attach an index card with step-by-step instructions for anything complex.

• Introduce your laundry system. Tell her how to handle spots; point out the detergent; talk to her about how you use bleach. Establish a place where family members place items to be hand-washed or treated separately. If you expect the children to put away their own laundry, tell her.

• Prepare a room-by-room checklist specifying what should be done in each room.

PLAYROOM CHECKLIST

At the end of the day:

—Have children put away what they can.
—Be sure toys get sorted properly (blocks with blocks; game pieces with correct game).
—Nap blankets should be refolded if children have used them while watching television.
—Art table should be cleared of everything except markers, crayons, and paper.

• Go over the lists and be clear about your expectations. Demonstrate how you like the beds made and how the children's rooms should be organized. If you won't be at home to teach all the details, try videotaping how you want each room to look.

• If your housekeeper is responsible for cooking, start her on simple recipes. Discuss any family likes or dislikes, and show her how to set the table and how you expect the kitchen to look after clean-up.

• If your caregiver does general cleaning or grocery shopping for you, make a separate list of her other household tasks and the day of the week you'd like her to accomplish them.

• Before establishing a full household schedule, take into account the number of children you have and how much time your employee will spend supervising their activities.

STEP FIVE: MAKING AN ASSESSMENT

As you and your new employee settle into a routine, you may find yourself saying, "Well, nobody's perfect . . ." That's true. Here are some suggestions to help you evaluate when "less than perfect" just won't do:

• If the issue is one of safety or dishonesty, or if she shows poor judgment (e.g., leaving the children alone while she runs to the store), let her go immediately.

• Use the "Five-Minute Rule." If something wasn't done as you like it, simply straighten it out yourself—if it takes no more than five minutes.

• If she's been with you for a time and suddenly things aren't going so well, consider: Is she having personal problems? If so, will they pass? Has the household schedule changed (e.g., toddler no longer napping)? Ask if she has ideas as to how problems can be solved. If not, you may need to make suggestions.

• After discussing a problem, give her a week or two to see if she can change the behavior.

• Provide opportunities for her to present her viewpoint.

• To avoid possible disputes, keep accurate records of payments made, and note sick days off.

• It's not working out when:

—The children don't like her.
—She's chronically late.
—She has sudden mood changes.
—You're constantly picking up after her.
—You and/or your spouse feel uncomfortable around her.
—You are reluctant to tell her what's on your mind.

While many parents fear the disruption in making a change, most find that replacing early and starting with someone new is preferable in the long run.

LIVING WITH A LIVE-IN

• Your relationship will be best if you set up the household so that you can be friendly without being intimate. If the employee is given a bed, a television, an easy chair, and perhaps a table or desk, it permits her to have personal time without having to join the family for a favorite television show.

• If your nanny is arriving at your home for the first time after a long trip, greet her, offer food and refreshment, and show her to her room. If she's up to it, a brief tour of the house or the neighborhood, perhaps conducted by the children, is enough for the day of arrival. If she has come in from overseas, give her the next half-day off to help her overcome jet lag.

• Establish rules concerning smoking, drinking, visitors, and use of the car.

• Discuss meal times. Will the nanny eat early with the children, or does the entire family, including her, eat together? Will there be exceptions when the family has company?

• Don't impose by asking her to "pitch in" during nonworking hours.

• Respect the nanny or housekeeper's private space, and teach the children to do so as well.

5

CHORES

WHAT'S AHEAD

Deciding What to Delegate

Assigning Chores and Keeping Track

Teaching the Chore

Getting It Done

Sticking with It

Children have many "jobs" during childhood—academic studies, social skills, physical achievements, and good, hard play. Learning responsibility through chores needn't be a large part of their day, but what they will gain through being a contributing member of the family is a sense of dedication and self-worth that will last a lifetime.

DECIDING WHAT TO DELEGATE

• Determine what the family chores are. Make a list of tasks to be done daily (making bed, clearing table, washing dishes) and another list of those done weekly (vacuuming, dusting, etc.).

• Consider your children's capabilities:

Ages three to five. At this age children are capable of one-step tasks (wash carrots; put blocks in bin) with a parent present.

Ages five to nine. School-age children can take responsibility for chores such as making their beds, but they will be more successful at other chores if you are nearby. Assign tasks that take ten minutes or less, or break a big chore down into ten-minute chunks.

Age ten and older. This age group is capable of working alone to perform more complex tasks, such as helping with siblings or doing an errand for you. Give specific instructions, and check on them occasionally.

• Schedule a family conference, and let the children voice an opinion on chores they would like to do. Your son may hate cleaning but not mind helping with meal preparation, and a positive attitude will increase the likelihood of success.

• Delegate according to preference and ability. Keep in mind that the most successful chores are "real" chores—the ones where the children see a benefit: If I scrape carrots, we eat them. The least successful are those with a remote benefit: Dusting may make a difference to you, but not to most children.

ASSIGNING CHORES AND KEEPING TRACK

Job charts and check-off methods provide an organized system for assigning what must get done.

Permanent Schedule

If you anticipate that jobs will vary only with the day of the week, here is a good chart for your family:

	Mon.	Tues.	Wed.	Thurs.	Fri.	Sat.	Sun.
Mom	dishes	trash	dishes	trash	dishes	trash	dishes
Dad	trash	dishes	trash	dishes	trash	dishes	trash
Julia	feed dog	feed dog	feed dog	feed dog	feed dog	feed dog	feed dog
Harrison	toy pickup	table	toy pickup	table	toy pickup	toy pickup	FREE
Joy	table	toy pickup	table	toy pickup	table	table	FREE

Job Wheel

Make a job wheel by cutting out two circles, one larger than the other. On the larger circle, write the chores; on the smaller one, note the names of all family members. Put the two circles together using a brad (available at stationery stores). Every day the smaller dial is moved one position to the right, making each family member responsible for new tasks.

Job Drawing

Write chores on separate slips of paper that are put in a bowl. (With this method, chores specific to the week can also be listed: "Buy get-well card," or "Wrap Grandma's present.") Once a week, family members draw to see what chores they have to do that week. This system works best when your children are old enough to perform a variety of tasks.

Job Pockets

On slips of paper, write family chores. On envelopes, write the names of family members. (Post these on a bulletin board or poster board.) These "pockets" will hold each person's daily assignments. Jobs can be requested, drawn, or assigned. As each task is completed a slip can be removed, giving you a quick way to check on whether certain tasks have been accomplished.

TEACHING THE CHORE

Explain chores thoroughly.

SMART TIP! *Step one: Break the chore down.* A chore such as "wiping the kitchen counter" sounds simple, but you'll quickly learn otherwise when you watch a typical eight-year-old grab a soaking sponge from the sink, drip water across the floor, swipe the sponge across the counter, pushing crumbs onto the floor and leaving water in the sponge's wake. Break *any* chore down into steps. Wiping a counter might involve: remove dishes; wring sponge out over sink; use sponge to brush crumbs neatly into cupped hand held at edge of counter; dump handful of crumbs into trash.

Step two: Demonstrate the chore exactly the way you want it done—down to the last detail. Show children how to bag garbage *and* how to use the twist-tie.

Step three: Supervise the chore, making helpful but noncritical comments: "Good job, but next time, try sweeping the leaves into the bushes instead of the driveway."

Step four: Increase responsibility. Let them do the chore when you're not around, or add one new step. (Bring in the milk and eggs from the milk box *and* put the eggs into the egg container in the refrigerator.)

Step five: Praise them regularly and often.

IMPORTANT! • If equipment is used in a chore, make certain it's child-appropriate and easy to use.

• Many chores can be done in just a few minutes. Show them how it can take five minutes or less to put books away, set the dinner table, wipe the bathroom sink, put folded laundry in the drawer, address a birthday card, rewind a rented videotape, etc.

• Don't redo a chore. This communicates a lack of trust and gives the child the feeling that his efforts are ineffectual.

"CLEAN YOUR ROOM!"

"Clean your room!" is one of the most frequently demanded chores by parents, but consider this from a child's standpoint. *Exactly* what does that mean? They need to be shown what the family standards are in the room-cleaning business.

• Start working with them when they are preschoolers, demonstrating how books are to be put back on the shelf; how only blocks go in the block bin, how dress-ups go in the basket.

• Point out what is being accomplished and why. "If we put your action figures away, you'll know where to find them tomorrow."

• Instead of saying: "Clean your room," be specific: "Would you please put your laundry in the hamper and make your bed."

• Has the mess in your child's room become overwhelming? Maybe your child is overwhelmed, too. Even a teen may need you to come in to help outline what needs to be done.

GETTING IT DONE

• Give young children transition time. "In a few minutes we're going to have to pick-up."

• Offer a limited range of choices: "Would you like to put away the puzzles or the stuffed animals first?"

• Set up a "star" system. Give a star for every day that all chores are completed, with a trip out for ice cream when seven stars are earned.

• Offer incentives. If your daughter wants to go to the playground, promise that you'll go, "after you've finished your chores."

• Make chores fun. For little ones:

—Clean up to music.

—Pick up toys around the house by giving your child a wagon, cart, or basket, and sending her on a "toy hunt."

—Race each other: "I can put away the books faster than you can put away the blocks."

—Let them be the parent; they can assign a task to you and choose one for themselves.

—Play a guessing game such as What's Out of Place? You might take a photograph of your child's room when it looks terrific. Mount or frame it. Then your child can examine the photo and compare it with "real life," noting what areas need picking up.

—Pretend. As a Ninja Turtle, your son could use his ingenuity to locate stray toys throughout the house.

• With older children:

—Be respectful of their other activities. Don't schedule chores during their homework time, or expect them to undertake a major task just before they're going out.

—Set a deadline. One working mother leaves "chore" cards for her young teens, and they know they are to be finished before she gets home from work.

STICKING WITH IT

After begging to do a chore, children quickly recognize a chore for what it is—WORK! Here's what to do when enthusiasm begins to wane:

• Let your children know that, as family members, they are accountable for chores. They should learn: "You don't have to like it; you just have to do it."

• Older children may ask for a reprieve or postponement. If it is negotiable, agree on a time when it must be completed, and hold them to it.

• Pay? If you want to, but only for chores above and beyond what other family members are contributing.

• Teach consequences, linking them as closely as possible to what was left undone. If your child fails to rake the leaves and you have to do it, then you may not have the time to take him to the video store on Saturday. (A child should be warned of the possible penalty.)

6

EMERGENCIES

WHAT'S AHEAD

Emergency Telephone Numbers

In Case of Emergency: Preparations for a Sitter

Emergency Consent Form

At no time is organization more important than in an emergency. Take time to prepare NOW:

EMERGENCY TELEPHONE NUMBERS

• Make one emergency list to be photocopied and posted at your main telephone upstairs and downstairs. Note numbers for:

Fire _____

Police _____

Poison Control Center _____

Ambulance _____

Electric company emergency number _____

Gas company emergency number _____

Pediatrician _____

Pediatric dentist _____

Pharmacy _____

Veterinarian _____

Work numbers—Mother _____

Father _____

Neighbor who would help _____

In-town relative to notify _____

Taxi _____

Nearest hospital and address _____

_____

Each child's name, birthdate, and blood type:

IN CASE OF EMERGENCY: PREPARATIONS FOR A SITTER

• Prepare an emergency envelope, and leave it in a designated spot. It should contain:

—Emergency money (for cab fare, gas, etc.). Include at least four quarters for telephone calls.

—Extra copy of your emergency numbers.

—Two index cards with clear instructions:

    1. Name of hospital, phone number, and exactly how to get there, and location of the emergency entrance.

    2. Pediatrician's name, address, phone number, and directions to the office.

Name _____

Birthdate _____ Blood type _____

Date of last tetanus toxoid shot _____

Allergies (particularly any to medication):

Chronic or past illnesses:

Health insurance company and ID # _____

Name of blood bank (if your family participates):

—Emergency consent form, leaving your most often-used sitter as the designated person in charge. (See sample below.)

—Also include a card with information on each child:

• Review the contents of the envelope with any new caregiver or evening babysitter. In an emergency, instruct them to take the entire envelope with them.

• Make a copy of all material in the emergency envelope to create a second envelope to keep in the diaper bag at all times. Should an emergency occur at the playground, you or your caregiver would have all the information necessary.

EMERGENCY CONSENT FORM

In case you cannot be reached, the person who is caring for your children should have a notarized letter from you giving over temporary medical authority. Prepare one for your mother if she's in charge for a weekend; give one to your nanny if you work outside the house. See the sample on the next page.

Remember:

• If your child has a health problem and regularly sees more than one physician, list those names and numbers as well.

• Because the form needs to be notarized, do this in advance if you're going to be out of town.

AUTHORIZATION FOR EMERGENCY MEDICAL CARE

Date _____

Name of Child _____

In the event that my child needs immediate medical attention and we cannot be reached, I/we give authority to _____ to request appropriate medical care for him/her. If our regular pediatrician is unavailable, then the pediatrician on duty at the hospital may provide or obtain medical care for my child.

Signed _____
(mother)

Signed _____
(father)

Mother _____ Phone _____

Father _____ Phone _____

Pediatrician _____ Phone _____

Notary signature _____

7

THE FAMILY CALENDAR

WHAT'S AHEAD

Setting Up

Using It Effectively

The family calendar is the key to coordinating family activities. If you have one place where you record dates and commitments, you'll know where everyone is supposed to be at any given time, and you can toss the scraps of paper the information was previously scribbled on.

SETTING UP

• Buy a wall calendar large enough to contain full notations on the family's comings and goings. A good-sized one measures 17″ × 22″.

• Hang it near a telephone so that when someone calls with a carpooling question or a date change, you can readily see whether or not the new suggestion will be convenient for you.

• Near the calendar hang a pen or pencil on a cord

so that you'll always have something with which to write. Note the initial of the person to whom the calendar notation (lesson, dentist appointment, playdate) refers, and write neatly!

USING IT EFFECTIVELY

• On the family calendar note *all* activities for each of your children as well as parental activities as they pertain to the family (carpooling and school volunteer responsibilities, business trips, and dates—such as evening appointments—requiring special child-care arrangements).

TIME SAVER! • Next to a playdate notation or a doctor's appointment, write down the appropriate telephone number in case you need to check on something or confirm.

• In your personal calendar, you'll also want to keep track of all family commitments so that whether you're at work or at home, you can tell at a glance what the day holds for everyone. Make a date with yourself (Sunday evening is a good time) to compare calendars at least once a week. Be sure that all pediatrician appointments or weekend dates you noted in your personal calendar while at work get transferred to the main family calendar. Likewise, all family calendar notes should be put into your personal calendar.

• Last but not least, don't forget to check the calendar each morning. A client recently told me: "I arranged for my daughter's piano teacher to pick her up for her lesson since I knew I couldn't bring her. Imagine how embarrassed I was when the teacher rang the doorbell, and my child wasn't ready! It was right there on the calendar. I just hadn't remembered to look!"

8

HOLIDAYS

WHAT'S AHEAD

Early Preparations

Holiday Planning

Gift Shopping

Wrapping and Storing Gifts

School Vacation and Working Parents

In December

Saying Thank You

Ending the Holidays in Style

For families, the holiday season ushers in a rush of school events, parties, entertaining, lots of relatives, and, of course, gift buying. Any smart holidayer will tell you that the best preparation is year round. Here's how to get started:

EARLY PREPARATIONS

• During the summer take family photographs to send with your holiday card (or to use as gifts for grandparents). The weather is dependable, and the children's faces won't reflect the stress of being corralled in December for the dreaded Holiday Picture.

• Establish a "Holidays" file folder, or purchase a notebook in which to keep:

—holiday card list
—gift list (current and past so you don't duplicate)
—list of monetary gifts given (note amounts)
—holiday craft ideas you find during the year
—new holiday recipes to try
—notes of things to remember for next Christmas: size of tree, where you've stored the tree stand, etc.

HOLIDAY PLANNING

WORTH THE TIME! • In early November, make a list of all the upcoming holiday tasks to be done; note who will be responsible and by what date. Set early deadlines—wrapped gifts can be tucked away; baked goods can be frozen—and mark them on the calendar. If the list is overwhelming, review it and cross out what you can.

• Write on the family calendar any school concerts or performances. Also, consider how you want to help out at school. Baking? Donating juice? Doing a project? By letting your child know now, you have a better chance that the tasks assigned fit the time you'll have to devote to them.

• Select major family activities (seeing *The Nutcracker*?

Sesame Street Live?) as soon as ads appear. Most parents find one or two special events is more than enough. Planning ahead also allows for an optimum experience, because the better seats are still available.

• Reconsider "day of" traditions in advance so that you'll have an opportunity to change them. Parents with a new baby and newly blended families need to take a particularly hard look at what they can reasonably expect from the holiday.

• Write *all* plans on the calendar, including traditional family activities. Also write down the afternoon you've chosen to decorate the tree and the day you promised the kids you'd make a gingerbread house. Even holiday television specials should be noted, or the time will slip away from you.

• As soon as any adult activities are scheduled, book your favorite sitter immediately.

• If you are considering a holiday trip, think it through carefully. Pediatrician's offices are filled with frantic parents who want their children's ears deemed "able to fly" or who are hoping that their child's fever is only a twenty-four-hour virus. This is a busy and germ-filled time of year. Planning a home-based holiday with the kids can often reduce parental stress.

• If you're among those families who do manage to travel at holiday time, set aside one suitcase as a "holiday bag." Keep it permanently packed with decorations or other specific items you like to have with you each year: children's stockings, red bow for the dog, etc.

GIFT SHOPPING

• Use last year's gift list to create this year's, and do it several months in advance. A few individuals start their new gift list as the current year's is put away.

MONEY SAVER! • Shop all year round. Find a great gift on sale? Buy it in multiples. Or if, in September, you have a wonderful idea for a holiday gift, put it on your "to do" list to pick up right away. Then note on your gift list that you have these items on hand.

TIME SAVER! • Shop by mail! You avoid traffic and hassles, and can call, fax, or mail your order in at your convenience.

• If you do have to shop near the holidays, hire a sitter so that you can do it alone. You'll work faster and can get shopping for the children done, too.

• Does it still seem like too much to do? Consider instituting a holiday grab bag. All names are placed in a hat

---

SIMPLE HOMEMADE GIFTS

Jewelry box. Take a cigar or small gift box; line with felt, paint the outside, and decorate with glitter.

Bookmarks. Use paper or cloth and choose a decorating method appropriate to your child's age.

Stationery. Buy regular envelopes and cut or purchase card stock to size; let the children personalize it with drawings or their own form of monogramming.

Pencil holders. Wrap cans with paper or material and decorate.

A poem, a story, or short essay about a grandparent can also be lovely. If it's short, frame it.

and each person draws a name in advance. Then you can buy one lovely, thoughtful present for one family member rather than trying to do something small for many.

• Many families like to have the children make gifts for grandparents or teachers. This can be as simple as a painting done at school or as complex as a special sewing project. Watch year round for potential ideas. Remember, too, it needn't be perfect.

WRAPPING AND STORING GIFTS

• Wrap gifts as you buy them. Using a detachable label, mark what is in each package.

• For hiding your children's presents, set aside as many large boxes as you have children. Mislabel the boxes as to content (e.g., "Extra Bedding"), and put them on a high shelf in closet, basement, or garage. A quick peek in the boxes will let you see whether the children have been provided for equally.

• If you stuff Christmas stockings, establish a transparent bag for each child, and use it to store the small items you pick up. You'll quickly see when you've reached a logical limit.

SCHOOL VACATION AND WORKING PARENTS

• If you work full-time, lack full-time help, and won't be able to spend the entire vacation at home with your children, plan carefully so that you needn't worry about how they are faring.

• Evaluate exactly when you and your spouse will be

off and determine what kind of coverage you'll need. If you take different days off (or one of you goes in early and the other late), you may be able to piece together more child care than you would expect.

• Team up with another family whose children your kids like. You may be able to cover the whole vacation among the four parents. If not, you could split the cost of a temporary sitter.

• Local Y's and some specialty schools (dance, gymnastics) often run special programs during long vacation periods. Look for one that fits your schedule and your child's interests.

IN DECEMBER

• In preparation for the new toys your children will receive, ask them to sort through their old ones. Broken toys and incomplete games should be thrown out; "gently used" items should be donated. In my family we pass around among cousins items such as tricycles, bikes, and dollhouses so that they needn't be stored and are always being used by someone.

• Establish family rituals that help move the holiday along but can become fun activities to do together. Children love to help with tree decorating, party preparation, gift-wrapping, and other holiday activities.

• Enlist help and use outside services to lighten your load:

—Hire a helper (a neighborhood teen?) to address Christmas cards, run to the post office, put up outdoor decorations.

—Bring in pizza on the night you're baking Christmas cookies.

—Team up with friends for holiday baking. Each of you prepares your own holiday favorite in multiples; then trade.

—Many companies now offer packing services. You give them the presents, and they pack and send them for a fee.

—If you can easily box things at home, then use package services such as UPS and request that they pick up the packages from your home.

—Simplify family gatherings by asking everyone to bring a dish, or consider using outside services for side dishes and desserts.

—If you have a new baby or are really feeling overwhelmed, ask that relatives give you the best gift in the world: extra hands. Maybe you'd love the house to be cleaned or perhaps you want time off to go to a movie.

ORGANIZATION PLUS! • For holiday outings, a large tote is indispensable. Use it to hold coats (roll them) and to store umbrellas, hats, and mittens. Tuck the tote under your seat and enjoy the performance without worrying that your little one may have kicked the umbrella out into the aisle.

• To help children cope with waiting, use the family calendar for a holiday countdown, crossing off each day as it passes.

• Slow down. If you find yourself getting frazzled, sit down immediately with the calendar. Evaluate what you can cancel and what you can live without.

IMPORTANT! • Schedule "Mother breaks." In most households, if Mom's energy fizzles out, the household falls apart. If you want a quiet evening to read, put the kids to bed promptly and turn on the answering machine. Or book a sitter and meet a friend for coffee.

SAYING THANK YOU

• The night before packages will be opened, take a pad of paper and write each family member's name on the top of a separate page. As the gifts are opened, note gift and giver on the appropriate page. After the festivities, each person will have his or her own list of people to thank.

• Children under age six will probably need to send a drawing in lieu of a note; older children ought to be able to write notes for themselves. Children between ages five and seven may be able to write their own notes if you provide a form for them to copy:

Dear _____,
Thank you for the _____. I love it.
Love,

• Ask your children to complete one or two notes per day until they have finished the task. Show them how to cross off each name on their list after the person has been thanked.

ENDING THE HOLIDAYS IN STYLE

• All holiday accessories should be stored together and carefully labeled. Enlist the help of all family members—if they are old enough to help decorate, they are old enough to help take down decorations. Note anything that should be replaced. You may be able to buy it now on sale, or make a note of it in your Holiday file so that you can take care of it early next year.

MONEY SAVER! • Shop the sales. Ribbons, paper, and cards bought at half-price can be stored with your other holiday decorations.

• Make note of what worked and what didn't work this year. What kind of tree did you buy? How tall was it? How many Christmas cards did you send? How many photos? Note any scheduling changes you'd like to make for the next year.

• Update your Christmas card list, adding new names and deleting those people with whom you've lost touch.

SMART TIP! • Take an afternoon or evening to organize next year's calendar. You'll need the children's school calendar and notations about any upcoming commitments of which you're aware. Transfer all upcoming events to the new family calendar. Add in weekly plans such as lessons, all birthdays and anniversaries, and other special occasions you'll want to remember.

PROCRASTINATION:
Raising Children Who Don't!

WHAT'S AHEAD

How to help children who procrastinate when:

They Don't Know How to Do Something
Their Work Habits Are Not Well Developed
They Fear Failure
They'd Rather Be Doing Something Else

Like adults, children feel stress when they procrastinate. Who really wants to be working on a school project at the last minute? They also experience disappointment when they put off practicing their swimming strokes, little understanding that practice is the "ticket" to obtaining a coveted berth on the swimming team.

Generally, children procrastinate for four reasons:

1. They don't know how to do something.
2. Their work habits aren't well developed.
3. They fear failure.
4. They'd rather be doing something else.

When you help your children overcome procrastination, you are actually providing them with a complete set of tools for planning and navigating their way through life. Here's how to help under various circumstances.

THEY DON'T KNOW HOW TO DO SOMETHING

• When your son is staring at his math homework instead of doing it, perhaps it's because he doesn't know how. You can solve this type of procrastination by getting him the help he needs.

SMART TIP! • Show children how to identify what the steps are for reaching a major goal. Does your daughter want to become a champion tennis player? An attainable first step is taking lessons and qualifying for the local tennis team. Here's how:

1. Call tennis teacher for schedule of lessons.
2. Coordinate preferred lesson time with the rest of the family's schedule.
3. Register, and send in payment.
4. As the lessons progress, your daughter should begin to ask about team requirements and tryouts.

By doing this, it gives you both a step-by-step blueprint for getting from here to Wimbledon.

THEIR WORK HABITS ARE NOT WELL DEVELOPED

• When it comes to tasks such as chores, what you perceive as procrastination may simply be that children don't automatically incorporate household responsibilities

---

HELPING BY OFFERING INCENTIVES

Depending on the child, you may want to set up incentives for reaching small goals on the way to a particular milestone. A child having trouble reading may find that the thrill of being able to do it herself is reward enough. However, if you feel she needs greater incentive, you might offer a sticker for each book read, with the promise of a special lunch for the two of you if she reads fifteen books during the summer. To set up a successful reward system, outline:

—Exactly what must be accomplished to qualify for the reward (chores must be remembered, homework turned in on time).

—Be specific as to the reward. Not: "I'll take you shopping." But: "I'll buy you one of those T-shirts you've been begging for."

---

into their lives the way adults do. Parents often wonder how a child can possibly forget to sweep the porch—he *knows* he's supposed to do it every Saturday. To children, that's not the sort of thing that's really worth remembering. Try a reminder system. Chore charts and check-off lists can help get the job accomplished.

• Teach your children to do difficult tasks during their "prime time." Are they larks (at their best in the morning) or owls (at their best later in the day)?

• Having a concept of time permits children to better plan for accomplishing chores or projects. From nursery school on, start pointing out to your children how long it takes to do a certain household task, how long a soccer game lasts, or whether their favorite television program is thirty minutes or an hour. This will begin to provide children with skills for understanding what can be accomplished in five minutes, twenty minutes, or an hour.

• Getting started on a project is usually the hardest. Teach these ways to get going:

1. Don't wait for a big block of time. They don't come often, even for children.
2. Start with the hardest task first. Everything else will seem easy.
3. Work in short spurts. If departure for baseball practice is delayed a half hour, show your child that he could use the time to advantage by: a) finishing his homework so he won't have to do it later; b) writing three birthday thank-you notes; c) putting away his laundry.
4. Start a small part of a larger project. A child who is daunted by the thought of doing a "whole twenty-page research report" could start outlining the first part of his report or even just gather the research materials.

ORGANIZATION PLUS! • For a project that takes several sessions, teach your child to use the end of one work session to prepare for the next one. Children can do this with homework projects by devoting a few minutes at the end of one day to organize notes or materials for the next day.

• If your child needs help from you, establish a specific schedule. And remember, you are the consultant, not the boss.

• If a child is having continual difficulty, examine the situation. Is she constantly late getting ready to go to soccer practice? Maybe she hates soccer. Does your son love the trumpet but balk at practicing? Talk to the teacher. Maybe the assignments aren't appropriate, or perhaps there are too many distractions at home.

• **Discuss consequences.** What will happen if the job doesn't get done or the deadline isn't met? If it was a family deadline, then perhaps a privilege should be taken away. If he forgets his homework too many times, the teacher will handle it; maybe that's the lesson that will take him off the procrastinating track.

• Any good work schedule includes time to relax. Teach your child to build in time off.

THEY FEAR FAILURE

• Procrastinators frequently stall because they fear that what they do may not be perfect. Teach your children that making mistakes is okay, that trying is what counts. Point out times when you're not perfect either.

SMART TIP! • When something your child is doing goes wrong (cat he draws has three ears, math solution is wrong), teach him to ask: "Can it be fixed?" By demonstrating that mistakes can be corrected, you will help him or her overcome procrastination caused by a fear of failure.

• Compliment your child on work habits, not product.

• Once children get started on something they've put off, offer them encouragement so they'll follow through.

• Adopt a more relaxed attitude about life by trying to be less anxious yourself when things go wrong. The better you do at taking minor daily upsets in stride, the more easygoing your children will be.

THEY'D RATHER BE DOING SOMETHING ELSE

Many times children procrastinate because they simply don't want to do what they're supposed to. One mother complained that her daughter was a master procrastinator: "She dawdles while dressing and procrastinates about making her bed. Homework is done S-L-O-W-L-Y. When it comes to evening bathtime, she tells me there's no need, because who wants to be well groomed at seven P.M.?" For a gentle nudging, try the following:

• Make a game of it. A room might be easier to clean with a favorite tape playing in the background, or the porch furniture might get a little whiter if you tell your daughter that she's not scouring a porch chair, she's scrubbing a throne.

• Encourage pride of "ownership." If the child who always has to be nagged to set the table decides to do it early one day—complete with handmade place cards— praise and encourage him.

• Recognize creativity. The sibling who hates doing the dishes may come up with some interesting alternatives and:

—Hire a sibling to do it.

—Swap chores with another family member.

While this may not be what you intended when you assigned family chores, your child has shown great initiative in coming up with a solution so that the chore gets done, but not by her. Watch over the situation, and set limits. Older siblings are perfectly capable of taking this too far!

• Teach your child that sometimes it's okay to let yourself off the hook. Sure, it would have been nice to make a present for the teacher at the end of the year, but if it didn't get done, a lovely card will do.

10

ROUTINES: A.M.
Making the Mornings Manageable

Have you ever tried to feed a baby at a specific time so that you can get to an appointment? Have you ever tried to leave home with three children, three backpacks, three coats and hats, six mittens, six boots, and, with luck, three lunches in the backpacks of the right kids? (Oh, and don't forget the library books!) When kids are involved, it's rarely easy.

Here's how to get the whole family out of the house on time.

THE NIGHT BEFORE: PLAN AHEAD AND SIMPLIFY

• Make a checklist for the morning, noting appointments to be confirmed or items to be taken (library books, a child's show-and-tell item, cleaning, etc.). Have these laid out and ready to go.

• Lay out "leaving home" necessities: your own briefcase, transportation money or ticket, and, depending on the weather, needed items such as gloves, boots, or umbrellas for all family members. The appropriate coats should be on nearby hooks or easily accessible in the coat closet.

• Establish a specific place for your keys and glasses to avoid a last-minute hunt.

• Repack and organize baby and toddler supplies and equipment each evening. Change carriage bedding and sterilize bottles for the next day.

• Repack the diaper bag. Did you use one or two diapers? Is the blanket dirty? Are you almost out of wipes?

• Plan your own outfit for the next day; prepare purse and briefcase.

• Organize your child's clothing the night before. To simplify:

—Limit your child's choices. Select two outfits, and then let your child choose between them.

SMART TIP! —Remove from sight all clothing that doesn't fit and put away out-of-season items.

• Prepare school notes and permission slips the afternoon or evening before. Put them in your child's backpack.

• Lunches should be prepared in the evening while

WHAT TO PACK IN A DIAPER BAG

1. Burp cloth
2. Diapers
3. Wipes and a small tube of diaper ointment
4. Pacifier (if used) and a toy or two—teething toys and rattles for babies; puppet or surefire toddler amusements for the older set
5. Bottles—take along an extra in case you get stuck or want to fill one with water
6. Tissues
7. Disposable plastic bags
8. Blanket
9. Change of clothing (keep permanently packed)
10. House key (a spare), emergency envelope (see Chapter 6), and extra cash

---

the family is fixing dinner (see Chapter 13). If the lunch requires refrigeration, add "take lunch" to your morning checklist. Otherwise, leave it on the kitchen counter.

• Run the dishwasher right after dinner and empty it later that night. Lay out the dishes you'll use at breakfast, and set the table for the morning.

THINKING AHEAD IN THE MORNING

To make morning activities automatic, establish a set routine for the whole family.

• Get up before the rest of the family so that you have a few minutes to get organized for the day.

• Put a clock in every room, even the bathroom. Advance your watch and clocks three to five minutes, or set a kitchen timer to help shorten a long shower or a detailed makeup routine.

• Employ teamwork. Some fathers wake and feed the children while mothers have an opportunity to dress uninterrupted.

• If you're the parent of an early riser, you will need to offer activities (special books or toys, a video) to keep your child busy while you get ready in the morning.

• Limit breakfast choices.

• Finish what you start:

—Make your bed right after you get up.
—Keep a sponge in the bathroom to do a quick mop-up after you've finished your morning routine.
—Do the dishes right after breakfast.

• Turn on the answering machine and screen calls.

• Try to allow an extra fifteen minutes of unplanned time to cope with the unexpected.

• If a last-minute problem occurs, or you're simply running late, there's still hope for a timely departure if you eliminate what isn't urgent. Just keep asking yourself, "Okay, what *must* be done now, and what can wait?"

MORNING ROUTINE WITH A BABY

• Review your morning schedule. Pick the elements that are most important to you, and then let the rest go or find other ways to get the tasks done. (Delegate to husband or caregiver?)

• If your baby takes an early nap, use that time to get dressed and take care of a few household chores.

• Keep a crawler in the room where you are and provide amusements. Finish in that room and move on together.

• Stow away a well-liked toy—or pack a small box with "irrcsistibles"—for that morning when you're desperate. You'll have the perfect amusement for a baby who gets restless before you're ready to go.

• Save "baby preparation" for last. Leave thirty to forty minutes for attending to the baby's needs. This provides time for nursing (or feeding) and should still give you the opportunity to pop him in a clean outfit and head out the door.

MORNING ROUTINE TODDLER-STYLE

IMPORTANT! • Help your child dress before breakfast.
• Stick with your own routine. Though you will likely find that toddlers will amuse themselves for short periods of time, don't be deluded. If you decide to make a phone call before you get dressed, you'll invariably regret it. A toddler's attention span can snap at any moment, and you'll still need to get ready.

• Make sure you know where your child's favorite blanket or teddy bear is before it's time to leave.

MORNING ROUTINE WITH A PRESCHOOLER

WORTH THE TIME! • Allow time for your child to dress himself. Self-dressing takes added time, so allow an extra ten minutes. Ideally, start letting him dress himself in the summer. Clothing is easier to put on, and families tend to have more time.

• Fight stubbornness with creativity. Children this age are looking for areas of control. Suddenly Jimmy is *not* going to put on his shoes, and Jessie refuses to have her hair combed. Humor ("Do your shoes fit on your ears?") and other forms of silliness may help get you through an impasse.

• Have your preschooler make her own bed. Teach your child to stand or sit at the very top of the bed and then pull up the sheet, the blanket, and then the top coverlet. (A comforter can cover up a multitude of wrinkles.) By climbing out of bed carefully, your youngster need only place the pillow on top to complete the task.

THE SCHOOL-AGE CHILD IN THE MORNING

• Use personal checklists for each child. Post them at a child's eye level on the refrigerator or on a kitchen bulletin board. Each child should be responsible for checking off the tasks as they are completed. For readers, the list can be in words; use pictures for younger children:

ANDREW

☐ homework in ☐ backpack; backpack by door
☐ teeth brushed
☐ hair combed
☐ dog fed
☐ bed made

• Delegate to your child. The kindergartner might amuse the baby; the eight-year-old can rinse a few dishes.

What you ask will largely depend on how much time the family has in the morning, and whether you are dealing with a slow or fast waker.

MOTIVATING THE MORNING DAWDLER

Some children are dawdlers from birth. Others go through stages when they endlessly dawdle. Whether you have a "lifer," or whether your child is simply going through a phase, here are some suggestions:

• Begin by planning extra time for "dawdler management." You may have to get up earlier, or reduce the number of things you expect to accomplish before leaving home.

• Build in dawdling time for him or her as well. Your dawdler may need forty-five minutes for breakfast, so plan for it.

• Provide your dawdler with a clock. You might try placing a clock radio (set to an upbeat station) on the other side of the room to help your sleepyhead get out of bed.

• Have breakfast ready so that after the dawdler is dressed, he or she can go immediately to the table.

• Eliminate distractions. Morning television and playtime should be permitted only after a child is dressed and ready for the day.

• Countdowns in five-minute increments help everyone prepare for a transition. (For the true dawdler, five-minute warnings may need to start fifteen minutes ahead.) Combine countdowns with "task" reminders for the younger child: "Five minutes until we leave. Please go to the bathroom now."

• Motivate your child to be ready to leave in time by

reminding him or her of something pleasant that is to happen that day. "Time to leave for school now, and, remember, the book fair is today!"

• Reminding your child that she will have to walk into the classroom after everyone is settled can sometimes be a great motivator.

• Take over. Some mornings you may not be able to allow him to tie his own shoes or pour his own milk. Spell those rules out ahead of time, so that the change of power doesn't have to be carried out in anger. "If you're ready on time, you may tie your own shoes. If we're running late, I'll need to help you."

• For the born dawdler, reward systems can sometimes help motivate habit change. Consider stars on a chart, a penny reward, or the promise of a special game in the evening for every time a dawdler is ready to leave on time.

11

ROUTINES: P.M.
How to Manage Evening Chaos

WHAT'S AHEAD

Coming Home

For Mothers Who Work Outside the Home

Dinnertime

The Evening Telephone

Bedtime Routines

In the reality of the nineties, I can't think of a single family who regularly enjoys a calm and easygoing evening! Women work, children's activities continue into the evening hours, and commuters often don't get home in time to have a sit-down family dinner. It's also the low-energy, high-stress time of day, when everyone is needy; most families call it the "witching" or "arsenic" hour.

Despite the hubbub, the family still needs to reconnect, and here's how:

COMING HOME—MAKING A SMOOTH TRANSITION

WORTH THE TIME! • When the children come home from school or you arrive home from work, expect to dedicate five to ten minutes to listening to each child. Limit interruptions. (If you're interrupted, it often leaves everyone feeling grumpy and dissatisfied.) Put on the answering machine, ask one of the children to take messages, or ignore the phone while you spend these immediate few minutes with the kids.

• Check homework before dinner, and avoid nagging or criticism.

• Maintain a regular evening schedule: homework, dinnertime, baths, and family time, for example. By developing a set routine, all family members know what to expect.

DINNERTIME

If you can't get everyone together seven nights a week, choose four nights and make a point of enjoying this time.

• Share responsibilities. Try letting one parent cook while the other focuses on the children. After dinner, reverse roles. If your spouse is gone on weeknights, have him or her be responsible for weekend meals. Otherwise, older children can help with almost all phases of dinner (planning, shopping, cooking within their ability), or help with a baby or toddler. The preschooler can do tasks such as getting out nonbreakable dishes, setting the table, washing lettuce and vegetables, and keeping you company.

MAKING THE TRANSITION:
FOR MOTHERS WHO WORK OUTSIDE THE HOME

- Use your evening transportation time to give yourself a break. By car, take a scenic route home; play favorite audiotapes; stop the car and read for ten minutes. By commuter bus or train, carry parenting magazines or a good novel.
- If you have an in-home caregiver:

    —Have her bathe the little ones before you get home.
    —Depending on your arrival time, you may want the children fed or dinner started.
    —Review any necessary details with the caregiver before she leaves.

- If you are picking up children at day care:

    —Give your children time to say good-bye to the teachers and any special friends.
    —Check with the day-care provider regarding any unusual occurrences of the day.
    —Have something in the car for them to look forward to—picture books, drawing materials, or stuffed animals. You might want to provide juice and a light snack, too.
    —Use time in the car as the perfect "coming together." You can talk or sing. In warm weather, stop at a playground for fifteen to twenty minutes to get some fresh air.

- Simplify the planning and cooking process:

—Establish certain dinners for certain nights. Spaghetti on Tuesdays and pizza on Fridays makes planning and shopping easier, and it gives the family a well-liked meal to look forward to.

TIME SAVER! —When you cook, make double amounts and freeze half. (Or try fixing several meals on the weekend and freezing them.)

SHORT-CUT! —Look for shortcuts. Try buying pre-sliced salad makings and ready-made foods such as microwave dinners.

—Plan a noncooking night (order in, go out, have leftovers) so that you can spend more time with the family.

• A headache-saver: Don't prepare foods you *know* your children won't eat.

• For picky eaters, allow one substitution—preferably one that they can fix themselves. Keep on hand a plate of healthy snacks (carrots, cheese, crackers, etc.) to use as a dinner substitute; older children can make themselves a sandwich if they don't like a particular meal.

• Before you sit down at the table, try to anticipate what might have you jumping up again:

—Seconds on drinks? Put a pitcher on the table. (Fill drink glasses half full to reduce the possibility of spills.)

—Does your baby always pitch at least one spoon off the table? Have spares on hand.

—Set the table with extra napkins.

• Children don't have the capacity to sit at the table for long periods, so excuse them when they are ready.

• Everyone should help clear the table. Even a five-year-old is capable of scraping a plate, putting it in the sink, and throwing out a napkin.

ORGANIZATION
PLUS!
• Before leaving the kitchen, organize the school lunches for the next day (see Chapter 13). Better yet, ask your spouse or one of the children to take responsibility.

THE EVENING TELEPHONE: FRIEND OR FOE?

There's no right or wrong way to handle the telephone in the evening. It depends on the age of the children and the nature of the household.

• Mothers of younger children generally prefer to make necessary phone calls at 7:30 or 8:00, after the little ones are in bed.
• Mothers of older children often like to make their two-minute carpooling and playdate confirmation calls near the dinner hour. (Lengthy calls are better made at other times.) A kitchen telephone with a long cord or a speaker will let you cut vegetables or pour glasses of milk while confirming details.

TIME
SAVER!
• If you're having a bad night, telephone calls are a terrible disruption. Ask one of the children to screen calls ("not interested" to solicitors; "she'll call back," to friends or business associates; "she'll be right with you," to the quick carpooling/playdate confirmation calls). If your kids are too young to serve as family receptionist, purchase an answering machine for the kitchen so that you can screen calls while fixing dinner.

BEDTIME ROUTINES

• Schedules work best if they are essentially the same seven days a week, so that a child gains a sense of a daily rhythm. While you may want to adjust the bedtime thirty minutes to an hour on a weekend, don't alter it greatly if you want the schoolday routine to be easy to maintain.

• Young siblings close in age should be bathed together; older ones, consecutively.

• Set a specific routine for brushing teeth so that it's done automatically.

• Anticipate what will have your kids jumping out of bed:

—Have them go to the bathroom before getting in bed.

—Put a glass of water by the bed of a child who frequently needs a drink.

—Set up a night light or provide a flashlight for a child prone to being frightened.

• Institute a time for them to be in their rooms for a quiet activity. Most families find reading together makes this transition time special, though talking, singing, or telling stories are also good ways to unwind.

• Too tired to read tonight?

—Let older children read to younger ones at bedtime. They develop their reading skills; the younger siblings like the attention.

—Let little ones thumb through a picture book.

• Most children develop rituals they count on—they want a kiss, a hug, and a song, in that order, without fail. Often this ritual becomes a twenty-five-minute ordeal. Let

MANAGING A CHANGE IN THE ROUTINE

Even if some nights are "perfect," it takes very little to throw an evening off-balance: a traveling spouse, a sick child, or a night out for Mom and Dad all throw the evening timetable out of whack. Here's how to cope with the unusual:

Plan ahead. If you know you're going out, make sure your fourth-grader is a night ahead on his research report; cook the night before; write out sitter instructions earlier in the day.

Set priorities. If the evening is careening out of control, start asking, "What *must* be done?" and do only the most important things.

Simplify. If you have some time, but not enough time, look for alternatives to your normal routine. Can you take a shortcut, or skip some chores? The kids can skim through the tub (or even skip a bath for a night); you can bring in fast food. What chores can you delegate?

Keep your sense of humor. There *will* be evenings when you come home and the stove isn't working and the telephone is ringing off the hook. These are the times when you bring in pizza and turn on the answering machine. In our house, no matter how bad things are at night, they always look better in the morning!

your child choose the three parts of the ritual that are most important, and drop everything else.

• Be consistent. If you are firm and certain in your response to "Five minutes more . . ." and "Just one more story . . . ," you'll save yourself a lot of bedtime bargaining.

• Consider your own needs. Allow for some personal time before you go to sleep.

12

SCHOOL:
Homework

Family stress over homework is legendary. Whether you're encouraging an overtired first-grader to take "just one more look" at the addition problems or demanding that your eleven-year-old turn off the television until after schoolwork is done, supervising homework can be very time-consuming for parents.

If you establish a specific homework routine for your children, the entire family will benefit. You'll save time, and your efforts will help instill in your children productive work habits and an organized approach to problem-solving.

THE SPACE

Set up a work area for your child, keeping in mind these features:

• *Central location* (for a young child). A table or desk in the family room or kitchen is ideal for the homework novice because it's easier for an adult to provide help and encouragement. Be careful that the location you choose doesn't have too many distractions. (You may still want to buy a desk for your child; it provides storage and will be used later on.)

• *Enough workspace in which to spread out.*

• *Good light.* Consider handedness when evaluating the light.

• *Chair comfortable for a child.* But if your child is a floor-sprawler and does her homework well, don't tamper with her method.

SUPPLIES

Remember the excitement of new school supplies? You can kindle enthusiasm for school by stocking a "homework office." Have on hand:

—backpack
—paper (lined and unlined)
—pencils (colored and regular)
—erasers
—pencil sharpener
—crayons
—markers
—ruler
—stapler

—glue

—tape

—calendar. As soon as the school sends out the calendar with vacations and event dates, help your child mark these on his or her calendar.

ORGANIZATION PLUS! —assignment notebook (small, perhaps $3'' \times 5''$). Particularly if the teacher has no organized method for giving assignments, teach your child to write down assignments here so that everything to be done will be in one place. Set up each page to record the following:

Date:

Assignment:

Due date:

Handed in:

—folders for homework

—storage file: accordion-style file folder with dividers for keeping schoolwork you plan to save. Label with child's name and date. (Ideal for reviewing progress.)

—2 dictionaries: one children's and one adult's (The children's dictionary is valuable for its simplicity and pictures. Kids often ask about words that aren't listed, making both books necessary.)

—atlas

—poster board. Keep 5 or 6 pieces on hand for making the often-assigned poster.

—20 to 30 old magazines (nature ones are best) for creating collages and for other assignments

• Older children will also need:

—thesaurus

—encyclopedia (Nice but not necessary. There's always the library.)

—computer (becoming more and more important)

• Visit an office-supply store and purchase some organizing aids to store items neatly. The smaller items can be kept in a school-supplies box or a desk-size carousel. The larger items should be on the child's desk. If your child will be working in the family room or kitchen, make space for supplies on a nearby shelf or use a rolling cart so everything will be close at hand.

YOUR ROLE IN THE PROCESS

Almost all schools have a back-to-school night early in the year. At this meeting find out:

• How will homework assignments be given?

• Are children expected to remember oral instructions, or will they have a homework book where assignments are written down?

• How much time should your child spend on homework each night?

• What is the parents' role in the process? Should errors be pointed out and corrected?

• What is the best way to contact the teacher if your child is having homework difficulty?

THE SCHEDULE

• Homework time should be structured and specific. Some children prefer to get their homework done right after school, but most kids like to relax first. Establish the best time according to your child's needs—preferably before dinner!

• Establish break times for the youngster who finds it hard to sit still. Set a timer for fifteen minutes of work time; then time a five-minute break; keep resetting until homework is complete.

IMPORTANT! • Don't interrupt your child during homework. Phone calls can be returned later, and if he forgot to do his morning chores, discuss it with him *after* homework is completed.

• If possible, plan to set a quiet tone by doing some work of your own (bill-paying, etc.) while your child works.

• On the days your child has no homework, maintain the routine by encouraging your child to use the time for reading (though there's nothing nicer than an occasional day off!).

GETTING IT DONE

• For children eight and younger, you, an older sibling, or a capable sitter need to be nearby in case help is needed.

• To begin, review the assignments, and suggest that your child start by doing the most difficult one first. Ask

your child to explain to you how he is going to proceed.
• If the assignment is to write a story or an essay, teach her to begin by talking it through. This helps clarify where the story is going, what ending will be best, and any kind of twist that needs to be included.

• Teach a child to skip difficult problems and come back to them. Later, if it's still too difficult, he can ask for help.

WORTH THE TIME! • Teach your child to break a long-term assignment into parts. Help your child assess the steps involved. For example, for a book report, the steps might include:

1. Select book.
2. Get teacher's approval.
3. Read book. (You can break this down further by specifying the number of pages to read per night.)
4. Write first draft of report.
5. Prepare cover.
6. Copy final draft.

Together, agree on personal due dates for each step; put them on the calendar.

ORGANIZATION PLUS! • Teach children the benefits of completing something early. Encourage your child to work on major projects at a steady pace, setting a personal completion date a day or so before the due date. This will help your child establish a positive, lifelong pattern for meeting deadlines.

• Teach older children how to best use their textbooks. Demonstrate how to preview a book, checking the table of contents and examining what reference information is available: maps? glossary? appendix?

• Help a child set reasonable goals. If your child is getting only four out of ten spelling words correct, she needs to focus on getting five right the next time, not getting a perfect score. The graph below can help her chart progress and show her how five right can lead to six, rather than either of you aspiring to an instant jump to a perfect ten.

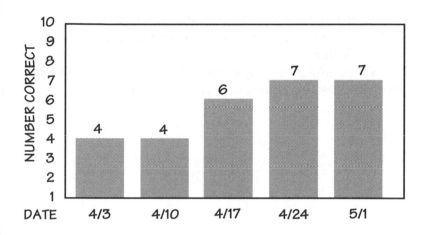

• Make sure your child places completed homework in his backpack upon completion. Monitor this practice until you're certain it has become second nature.

SUPERVISING HOMEWORK WHEN YOU'RE AT WORK

If you're not always home after school, set up a homework system that works even in your absence. Perhaps your sitter or nanny can supervise, or here are other options:

• Get together with other working parents and hire a high school student to supervise a "study hall" at someone's home.

• Establish a ritual whereby you can review homework with your child by phone. Ask:

—What are your assignments?
—Do you understand the instructions?
—What are you going to do first?

• Tell her that if she finishes before you get home, you'll have time to watch a favorite program or play a game with her.

• Once home, express interest in the homework and help with any final questions your child may have.

13

SCHOOL:
Lunches

WHAT'S AHEAD

Establishing a Lunch-Preparation Center

Shopping and Organizing in Advance

Packing It Up

When it comes to fixing school lunches, the watchwords are "kitchen convenience" and "assembly-line production." Here's how to make them work for you:

ESTABLISHING A LUNCH-PREPARATION CENTER

• Establish a shelf or a drawer in the kitchen where all basic lunch items can be kept to make the actual packing quick and efficient. You will need:

—lunch box or brown bags
—plastic bags
—napkins
—plastic utensils/containers

—juice or drink boxes
—favorite snack

SHOPPING AND ORGANIZING IN ADVANCE

• Purchase five days' worth of lunch ingredients on your weekly visit to the grocery store. Ask the kids for requests. You can easily prepare what they want so long as you have the ingredients in the house. Add to your shopping list or make sure you have on hand something to fill each of these categories:

—morning snack
—drink
—sandwich filling/crackers or bread or other main course such as yogurt, spaghetti, or soup
—fruit or vegetable accompaniment
—light dessert

SHORT-CUT! • If you use bags rather than a lunch box, take fifteen to twenty bags per child and label them with the child's name and class. Children ages seven and older can do it themselves. (Or invest in a personalized rubber stamp and have the kids stamp the bags.) Tell them they can decorate as many as they like, but only after they've written their name on the number you've specified.

TIME AND MONEY SAVER! • Pack your own "snack packs" to save money and reduce environmentally wasteful individual packaging. You and/or the kids can bag ten to twenty small plastic bags of pretzels, crackers, raisins, etc. (Ask your child to bring home the bags so that you can rinse and air-dry them to be used again.)

• If your child takes a lunch that can be frozen ahead of time (meat loaf, etc.), invest in five small containers, and pack a week's worth on Sunday night. Thaw night by night as the next day's lunch is packed. Your child can bring them home daily, and at week's end, you'll be ready to repack the five containers for the next week.

PACKING IT UP

• Pack lunch the night before.
• Lay out a labeled brown bag for each child and load them one at a time so that you don't mix which child gets what. Pack as follows:

1. Lay drink box flat on the bottom.
2. Place sandwich or main course item next.
3. Add plastic bags containing "extras" (snack, fruit/ vegetable, dessert).
4. Put in two napkins (one for lunch, one for snack), plastic utensils, and anything else your child needs.
5. Now and then, put in a surprise—a note, a sticker, a fancy napkin.

• Double-check the contents of each bag and refrigerate, if necessary.
• Children ages eight and older are capable of making their own lunches. If you decide to delegate this chore, help your child with it the first few times. Then spot check the packed lunch periodically to be certain that the bag isn't filled with chips and cookies.
• Put an adhesive-backed note on the inside of the front door, or leave yourself a note on the kitchen counter: "DON'T FORGET LUNCH!"

SHOPPING WITH AND FOR KIDS

When Julia was a toddler, our shopping expeditions would make my stomach churn as she tugged at the clothing, pulled garments off the shelves, and rearranged displays. "Leave her home" was always my plan for the next time. It's taken a few years, but now that she's seven, she's good company and a fine assistant. So, remain optimistic, hold on to your sense of humor, and follow this advice for smooth sailing down the shopping aisles.

BASIC GUIDELINES: PLANNING

• Whether it's a trip to the grocery store or a visit to the mall, create a very good list while at home. Write down all the items you need and the stores in which you intend to look for them.

• Avoid zigzagging around town. Plan an efficient route for making your purchases with a minimum of effort.

• Schedule your outing for an optimum time. Avoid peak store hours when lines are longest—5:00 P.M. anywhere, and Saturdays at grocery and department stores. Also consider your children's schedules. Avoid shopping when they are hungry or overly tired.

• Plan to shop quickly. You won't be able to bargain-hunt or search for the perfect birthday gift for your mother. That type of shopping should be done when you're alone.

• Use a stroller for as long as possible so that your child can see everything but still be physically contained.

BASIC GUIDELINES: PREDEPARTURE

• Pack emergency supplies. A juice box or bottle and some type of snack will fortify the weary or bored; take along a toy, a doll, or a book in case you must wait somewhere.

• Have your children go to the bathroom before you leave home.

• Explain to your children the errands planned and establish what your expectations are: "We need to stop at three stores. Please stay with me and remember not to touch."

BASIC GUIDELINES: THE EXPEDITION

• Praise your child for good behavior or for helping.

• Turn a boring errand into a fun game of exploration. Count the number of traffic lights you pass, recite rhymes, tell stories, or do word identification in signs you see.

• Is there a spot for a midway rest? An ice cream cone or a pause on a bench may help you get one or two more errands done.

• Have a tantrum-management plan:

—Quit before your child gets too tired.
—Discuss allowable treats ahead of time; don't give in.
—Think through how you will handle a "scene." Does your child respond to reasoning? If not, you may have to leave the store for a time.

• Plan to make your last stop the bakery or a place where you can buy your child a small treat. Or you might offer a trip to the playground if your mission is accomplished successfully.

ALTERNATIVES TO SHOPPING WITH KIDS

If you have three young children, a rambunctious two-year-old, or a very long grocery list, try to leave the children at home. Most parents don't want to hire a sitter specifically for errands or a grocery run, so here are some options:

• Shop at a time when your spouse can take care of the kids.

• Barter shopping time with a neighbor.

• Squeeze in errands at odd times. Pick up toiletries during your lunch hour. If an evening meeting for which you've booked a sitter ends early, get your grocery shopping done too.

• Delegate:

—Have your sitter or housekeeper do the grocery shopping, pick up the cleaning, or buy a get-well card. They may have extra time if your children are in school, and many are very savvy at shopping with kids along.

—Ask your cleaning help to be responsible for purchasing cleaning supplies.

—Older children can run some errands.

• Use personal shoppers. Some stores offer this as a regular part of their service.

• Patronize local stores that deliver.

TIME SAVER! • Shop by mail. From tulip bulbs and furniture to bed sheets and clothing, it's available in a catalog. Price-shop by comparing catalogs, and watch for sales—even mail-order companies have them! What if you don't like the item, or it doesn't fit? Reputable companies are very good about refunds. Simplify the return process by saving the packing materials until you're sure you're keeping the item.

• Shop while you're on vacation. You'll have more patience than you have at home, and you and your spouse can take turns watching the children. Take along your holiday gift list and tuck away what you buy. Also watch for outlet stores where you can buy everything for less.

SHOPPING FOR CLOTHES

• Sort through last year's clothing as well as the hand-me-downs, and locate those that fit and look fresh. Assess the clothing your children have, and list what they need.

• Scout the stores ahead of time so that you'll know exactly where boys' bathing trunks are, and where to find the best selection for your picky preteen.

• Shop early in the season to get the best selection, and avoid the shoe store the week before school starts! Parents of teens may want to *finish* shopping later in September. That way your child has the opportunity to see what is "in."

• Evaluate whether you need to take the children with you. (If they are fussy about what they wear or difficult to fit, you may have no choice but to take them.) Little ones will grow into anything reasonable, and boys usually don't care what you buy, so they are good stay-at-home candidates.

• Try taking one child at a time. Shopping is less frantic, and you can cap it off with a lunch together, making it a special time for you and your child.

• If you are taking the children, choose a store with a play area, and adjust your expectations—you won't be able to price-shop three stores or pick up makeup for yourself.

• Take along your spouse or a grandparent who can keep their eyes on the kids, keeping them nearby so you can check sizes.

• Make try-ons easy by having your children wear slip-on shoes and a two-piece outfit. (If you're only shopping for pants, your child's shirt or blouse can remain on.) Avoid layers, lots of buttons, or hard-to-zip jeans. Tie back long hair.

SMART TIP! • Buy it when you see it. If your daughter loves one particular blue dress, take it right to the cash register.

SHOPPING FOR GROCERIES

• For fast shopping, draw up a list of general categories (baked goods, dairy, fruit and vegetables, paper goods, etc.) according to store layout. Photocopy the list and have family members note needed items under the appropriate category headings. This way your list and the store layout coordinate.

• For little ones, buy a grocery-cart seat belt (available at children's supply stores). It keeps your child safe, and it's lightweight so you can carry it in your purse at all times.

• Do you have several children? Try getting one cart for the kids to push and one for you. (Put your baby or toddler in yours, and put the food in theirs.)

• Use children five and up to run in-store errands for you. As you turn into a new aisle, send them ahead (but still within view) to select items you need. Children who can read can keep track of the list for you.

MONEY SAVER! • Buy in bulk. Some families shop monthly, buying paper goods and the basics in quantity. When you have the children with you, make short fill-in shopping trips to specialty stores like the butcher or the fruit stand.

• You may find that two smaller trips to the grocery per week are easier to manage than one big one.

• Need just a few items? Keep baby or toddler in his or her stroller and work with a carry-all basket.

• For occasional items, shop in the smaller mom-and-pop stores where the lines are shorter and the space more confined.

15

SLEEPOVERS

WHAT'S AHEAD

First-Timers (Ages Five to Eight)
Seasoned Sleepers (Ages Eight to Twelve)
Slumber Parties

Sleepovers are a necessary rite of passage for youngsters, but ask other parents about these events and you'll hear of six-year-olds crying to go home in the middle of the night and of adolescents who think nothing of taking a Tarzan swing on the basement plumbing pipes.

Whether your child is guest or host, you want sleepovers to go well, so here's what I've learned about how to put the emphasis on fun—and on sleep.

FIRST-TIMERS (AGES FIVE TO EIGHT): GENERAL PREPARATIONS

• Let your child take the lead as to when he or she wants to participate in a sleepover. (However, postponing this "first" until age seven or eight helps assure success.) Most children talk with great enthusiasm about the possibility of a sleepover but are less enthusiastic when the time comes. Allowing a few weeks to pass from the time of the first discussion until the actual event is not too long. It allows time for a child to adjust to the thought of being away from home for the night.

• Read books like *Ira Sleeps Over* by Bernard Waber to your child to help him think through some of the issues surrounding being gone for the night.

FIRST-TIMERS: WHEN YOUR CHILD IS THE GUEST

• Schedule the first sleepover for a night when you'll be at home in case there is a problem.

• Talk to your child about adapting to other people's rules. You may not mind if the children bounce on the bed, but the other family may.

• Check with the host family in advance to see if a sleeping bag is wanted.

• Have your child choose which doll or stuffed animal to take. Offer reassurance: *Every*body—right up to teenagers—brings something along.

• Pack a utility kit: toothbrush, toothpaste, cup, comb, brush, soap with dish, lotion, powder.

• Fold self-contained outfits together. Send only one extra pair of shoes.

TIME SAVER!
• Tuck in a plastic bag for dirty clothing, and ask your child to place laundry in it.
• If sending special medicine, send it in a zip-lock bag with a spoon and written instructions inside.

• If your child has any allergies, health problems, or relevant habits (talking in his sleep?) tell the host family.

• If daytime playdates at the home of the sleepover are always supervised by a babysitter, then your child should have a little extra time settling in with the host-parents before you say good-bye.

• Tell your child when and if she may call home. For some children, it can help them through a rough moment; for others, hearing your voice may make the tears flow.

• If your firstborn is going for a sleepover, recognize that this may be a first for you, too. Both of you need to focus on the fun he or she will have; don't talk about how you'll feel when you see your child's empty bed that night.

FIRST-TIMERS: WHEN IT'S AT YOUR HOUSE

• Plan this for a night when you can spend time with them. The child who has played comfortably at your house during the day may be a little uneasy about a first night-time experience.

• Ask the parents if the guest has allergies, special needs, or food preferences.

• Remind the child to bring along a favorite toy, blanket, or stuffed animal. You might also suggest that the guest bring something fun to share like a favorite game or book. It gives them something extra from home and makes them feel special.

• Talk to your child about deferring to the guest when possible. Children who are gracious daytime hosts may still have difficulty sharing space and parental attention at night. If you can point out to your child that he will likely be given first choice at the friend's house, it may make it easier.

• Decide in advance with your child what the bedtime

will be. Allow for whispering time once the lights are out.

• Plan an involving activity like baking to keep the kids busy and to help the evening pass pleasantly. Being occupied helps stave off any feelings of anxiety.

• Give a tour of the house as it will be used that night: where the kids will sleep, where the nearest bathroom is, and where the light switches are.

• Assign to the guest a specific corner or a dresser top for belongings so they won't get misplaced.

• Explain to the kids what the evening's schedule will be: "After dinner we'll play a game, and then you can play until eight-thirty, when it will be time to get ready for bed."

• Keep things "exactly alike" to as great an extent as possible. Different-sized beds or beds of different heights may cause a dispute. To solve this, one family puts the mattresses on the floor to make the kids feel "equal." If that's not possible and the beds are viewed as unequal, then the child with the "least desirable" bed should get the "best" blanket, for example.

• Go overboard to make the child feel comfortable. If three extra pillows and another comforter will do the trick, then it's worth dragging out the additional bedding.

SEASONED SLEEPERS (AGES EIGHT TO TWELVE): GENERAL POINTERS

• Ritual sleepovers (a regular sleepover with one special friend) are good for this age group and can be very nice for both families. Because the kids know exactly what to expect, and because they know that the occasion will occur again soon, they tend to be accommodating guests in both homes.

• Schedule a sleepover at your house on a night when a sister or brother is sleeping elsewhere. It cuts down on confusion for you and is particularly special for the kids involved.

SEASONED SLEEPERS: WHEN YOUR CHILD IS THE GUEST

• By age nine or ten, children are usually quite self-sufficient in preparing for a sleepover (though you may want to suggest taking along a comb and a toothbrush). If you are lucky, your children will maintain your system of using a plastic bag for dirty clothing; if not, you can at least insist that they unpack afterwards and get their own laundry into the hamper.

• Explain to your child that the other family won't be mad at her if she asks that the cat—to which she's allergic—stay off her bedding.

• Inquire about who will be with them in the evening. By this age, some families schedule sleepovers on evenings when a sitter is there. You should be told that.

• It's best to end sleepovers by noon the next day. Even the best of friends are generally ready for some private time by late morning.

SEASONED SLEEPERS: WHEN IT'S AT YOUR HOUSE

SMART TIP! • Schedule an out-of-the-house activity such as going to a movie. The kids think it's a wonderful treat, and you benefit because they are less wound up when you arrive home at nine or ten and ask them to prepare for bed. (Sleepovers after children have spent the day at camp are also successful; the kids are tired enough to go right to sleep.)

• Indicate a dresser or corner for the guest to use to keep their belongings collected.

• Though the children will want a later-than-usual bedtime, set limits so that they aren't up all night. (Sleepovers need to work for the family as well as the children.) If your child and the guest defy you, you can easily express your displeasure by not allowing sleepovers for a time. They'll get the message.

SLUMBER PARTIES

By the time most children are nine or so, they've decided that the finest birthday party imaginable is the dreaded-by-parents SLUMBER PARTY. If you undertake this, here are some suggestions:

• Limit the guest list as much as possible, and do your best to see that the group is compatible. A three against one grouping for fifteen hours (6 P.M. arrival—9–10 A.M. departure) is a nightmare.

• You and your child should agree on a target sleep time. Unless you don't mind missing a night's sleep, you should make it clear that this is to be a *slumber* party.

• Schedule an activity (bowling, roller- or ice-skating) for the evening hours. It tires them, and gives the kids fewer hours to generate let's-stay-up-all-night energy.

• Have sanctioned snack food planned. That's part of the fun of a slumber party.

• Make sure you have phone numbers for all parents.

• Schedule an early pickup (nine or ten o'clock), but

have a specific low-energy activity planned for the early morning.

If you can keep a sense of humor and even view a slumber party as an opportunity to use some ingenuity, you may find there are ways to make everyone happy. One boy was adamant about having a sleepover for his eighth birthday, and equally adamant that he wanted to stay up all night. His mother devised a way around this: "About ten P.M. the boys went to the basement to watch videotapes and play," she explains. "I set all the clocks in our house four hours ahead. When they came up about twelve-thirty to see what time it was, they saw that the clocks said four-thirty A.M., and they were elated. They went back downstairs and promptly went to bed!"

16

SPACE MANAGEMENT:
Closets

In most homes I visit, the children's closets are a dumping ground for a miscellaneous collection of things. A baby's closet is likely to still hold parents' belongings, ranging from out-of-season clothes to skis. As children get older, the closet is turned over to them, but what a jumble—everything from odd slippers to unboxed Legos! Opening closets like these is definitely like opening Pandora's box.

Here's how to make your child's closet functional, orderly, and easy to keep clean.

THE WELL-PLANNED CLOSET IS:

• *Simple.* If something's easy to get out, it's easy to put away.

• *Accessible.* Your child should be able to reach everything you want him to without asking for help.

• *Innovative.* Be creative about storage: The back of a closet door can hold a towel rack where you hang scarves and ribbons; or hooks can hold bags, hats, pajamas, and a robe.

• *Flexible.* Don't overcustomize; a child's closet may need to go from holding a handful of toddler's clothes to storing reams of teenage finery.

THE PRACTICAL CLOSET

Most closets provide far more hanging space than children need. To better utilize the space:

• Divide the closet into two parts. One side will be for hanging clothes; the other will be for folded clothing, items stored in bins, and/or any other storage needs you have.

SPACE SAVER! • Double-hang (top bar and lower bar) on the "hanging" side. You can maintain the same amount of hanging space while bringing a rod down to a child's level. To add a lower bar:

—Use tension rods and place poles at the appropriate level.

—Buy a kit that provides you with the right materials to lower (and double) the hanging space (available through catalogs and at closet shops).

── CONSIDER SPACE AND STORAGE NEEDS ──

1. Consider the shape and size of your children's closets.
2. Consider your child's storage needs:
   —Do you already have a dresser, shelves, or built-ins that hold clothing?
   —Do you have adequate space in the room (or elsewhere in the house) for games and toys?
   —Is there space in the hall closet for items such as boots and outerwear?
   —Do you have a place in the garage, basement, or near the back door for storing sports equipment and outdoor toys?
3. Based on the above, what do you *need* to store in your children's closets? Check off below:

☐ blouses and shirts	☐ shoes
☐ dresses	☐ boots
☐ jeans, pants, and shorts	☐ coats, jackets
☐ sweaters	☐ hats
☐ pajamas	☐ rain gear
☐ underwear	☐ toys and sports equipment

    —Use a cord on either side to hang a dowel (long round pole available from lumber yards) to create a lower pole.

    • Put shelving in the other half of the closet. The items are visible and accessible while the closet door is open and out of sight and out of the way when the door is closed. Create shelves that are:

—Easy to adjust.
—Low enough for kids to reach.
—Well-sanded and splinter-free. Treat the shelves with a top coat of polyurethane to make them easy to wipe clean.

• Built-ins should be spacious and easily accessible. Some built-in units are modular and removable so that you can add to them when changing the closet or take them with you when moving to a new home.

• Wire mesh carts, available in home-furnishing shops, make for convenient lower-closet storage; shelves are added above.

• If you must store toys, games, and/or sports equipment in the closet, plan accordingly. Shelves can be spaced close together in one part of the closet to accommodate games or puzzles; a large bin can be added below for balls and bats.

• Install a light in the closet so that clothing is visible. A light that turns on automatically when the door is opened is ideal for kids.

• Buy child-size hangers. The cloth hangers designed for baby clothes can be replaced by junior-size plastic hangers available through catalogs and at closet shops.

• When using boxes for storage, choose transparent ones and label with name, contents, season, and size.

ORGANIZATION • Colored bins on shelves are perfect for PLUS! storage. Code them by color: perhaps undershirts in red, socks in yellow. It's easier to put things away, and when you ask your three-year-old to get his socks, you can remind him of the color of the bin.

• For shoes, buy or have built a simple shelf system that runs across the bottom or along the side of the closet. Shoes can be paired up and neatly put away.

• Keep a step stool in the closet so that you'll have a convenient way of getting to the higher shelves.

• Plan space for a hamper if you keep one in your child's room.

CLOSET RULES

• A place for everything, everything in its place.
• Put everything away daily; items that are dirty or need to be mended should go in the laundry or mending pile.
• Fold matching outfits together (including pajamas) and store on a shelf, or hang together on the same hanger.
• Keep the closet floor free of clutter.

CLOSET TRAPS

• *Shoe bags.* They collect dust and grit, and eventually the weight of the shoes causes the bag to tear.
• *Storing shoes on the floor.* They get kicked out of place and lost behind other things, and it makes for difficult cleaning.
• *Putting things away unlabeled or behind other items.*

MAINTAINING AN ORDERLY CLOSET

A major challenge in a child's closet is keeping the clothing pared down to the seasonally appropriate items that fit.

CHILDREN'S CLOSET

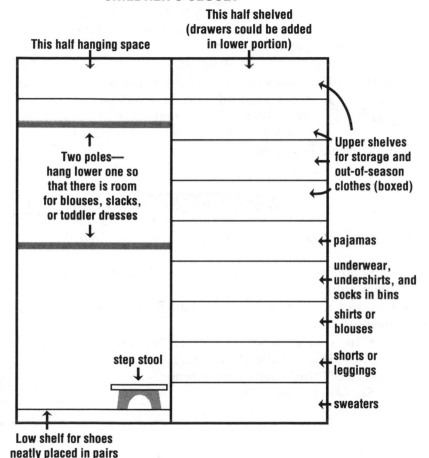

This half shelved (drawers could be added in lower portion)

This half hanging space

Two poles—hang lower one so that there is room for blouses, slacks, or toddler dresses

Upper shelves for storage and out-of-season clothes (boxed)

pajamas

underwear, undershirts, and socks in bins

shirts or blouses

step stool

shorts or leggings

sweaters

Low shelf for shoes neatly placed in pairs

• Set up an automatic system in your laundry area so that when something that is too small comes through, it gets washed and placed in a special box or bin. From there you can take it to the "donations" pile or to the box where you keep hand-me-downs.

• In the spring and fall, wardrobes must be switched.

As you sort, create two piles: One is clothing you know your child will have outgrown by the following year; put these with donations or hand-me-downs. The other pile is for clothing that is worth saving for next season. These items should be boxed, labeled, and stored on the top shelf of your child's closet until the seasons change again.

SMART TIP! • Sorting and labeling hand-me-downs is vital to being able to make use of them. Label boxes with name, age, and season for which the clothing is suitable.

A CLOSET FOR TWO

Set up separate storage space for each child.

• Double-hang in the middle of the closet with shelves down either side. Each child gets a side for shelved storage, and a shelf across the bottom can hold both children's shoes.

• In a wide closet, designate "his and her" or "her and her" sides of the closet. Each side should have rods, bins, boxes, and shelves for storage.

See also Chapter 19.

17

SPACE MANAGEMENT:
Clutterproofing Your Household

The messiest day in my home wasn't after a big party, on moving day, or even when my then two-year-old smeared cold cream all around her room. It was when our twins were born. While I was in the hospital, my loved ones went mad and left *everything* out: mail, dishes, toys, clothes, gifts . . . With all the excitement, who had time to pick up and put away? When I got home, I realized there was only one solution: I got into bed and pulled the covers over my head!

Under more normal circumstances, here's how to do it right:

TOY CLUTTER: WEEDING OUT

Children today have many more toys than we ever did. Here are three ways to artfully manage the clutter:

1. With little ones, go through their rooms twice a year, throwing away the broken, and sending to charity the unneeded or unloved.
2. Rotate. Pack up some of your child's possessions in boxes and put them away. When you unpack the boxes in a couple of months, your child will be delighted. (Now select a new group of toys to go into "retirement," and store them away.)
3. Inspire your children to have a yard sale. Let them organize it—and profit from it. (Of course, this clutter now becomes another parent's clutter!) Suggest they invite friends to join in and sell their things, too. Recommend that the children take the following steps:

CLUTTER MANAGEMENT: ESTABLISHING RULES

• Establish rules to manage bedroom clutter:

1. No food in the bedrooms. (Even better: no food outside the kitchen or family room.)
2. No dangerous items on floor. (Always put away loose balls or roller skates.)
3. Laundry must always be put in the hamper.

• Establish a specific clean-up time. The frequency depends on your style:

HOW TO HAVE A YARD SALE, KID-STYLE

—Select toys to be sold.

—Clean items; add ribbons to stuffed animals.

—Set prices (consider young budgets). Instead of tagging everything, have the children create boxes to hold 25-cent, 50-cent, or $1 items.

—Seize the moment! If the children become enthusiastic on Wednesday, let them have the sale Saturday. (Be sure a parent can be on hand.) They can phone friends, or send "runners" to houses to announce the ongoing sale. As a last resort, they could take a wagon-load of things to a nearby playground to see if there are any takers.

—Have kids make and put up posters.

—Help them bake cookies or brownies to sell to "lookers."

—Have plenty of change on hand.

1. As-you-go-along pickup: You may want each toy or puzzle put away before your child takes out anything new.

2. End-of-the-day pickup: This gives children freedom while still providing for a fresh start the next morning.

3. Biweekly pickup: Have them clean up two or three times per week, which permits them to keep something special (like a massive block fort) out for a few days.

• Are friends expected to help pick up? Including them teaches cause-and-effect: If you pull down all the stuffed animals, you have to help pick them up.

COMING-HOME-FROM-SCHOOL CLUTTER

When children arrive home from school, they "moult" instantly: backpacks, coats, sweaters, mittens, and hats slide to the floor; shoes or boots are tossed; and a pile of "things" are left to be stepped over. Here are solutions:

• Coats, jackets, or slickers should be hung up as the children come in. Hang child-accessible hooks in the hall closet, or place a child-size coatrack near the door.
• Return mittens to coat pockets or place with other accessories (hats, scarves, gloves) in a basket or bin near the door.
• Establish a specific place for backpacks.

One mother solved her family's coming-home clutter problem by having a carpenter build a seat in her back entryway. Three good-sized drawers (one for each child) were constructed underneath. When her children come home, coats go on hooks, and mittens, hats, and backpacks (after they're emptied), are all put into the appropriate drawer until the next day.

SCHOOL-PAPER CLUTTER

From the moment your three-year-old starts nursery school, you're in for a paper blizzard. Here's what to do:

SMART TIP! • As the children empty their backpacks, ask them to give you permission slips and important notes. Process them immediately and put them right back into the child's backpack. (If you can't do it right then, establish an envelope for them until you can process the papers later in the evening.)

• File, or have your child file, anything you want to save (report cards, special certificates, etc.).

• If you can do it without being seen, toss out some of their school papers that evening—you don't need to save every worksheet and painting your child produces. Save all other papers in an accordion-style file folder complete with dividers (organize papers by subject) or an oversized art portfolio, perfect for a collection of younger children's things. At the end of the year, weed out one more time and put the file/portfolio in storage, marked with the child's name, the year, and the grade.

CLUTTER CONTROL: A QUICK FIX

It's been a hectic week, and the house clutter is driving you nuts, but you have only an hour on Sunday to straighten up before the next Little League game. For a quick redo:

• Call a hasty family meeting, and ask each family member to help. Little ones may be capable of working for only ten minutes, but, at this point, anything is a help.

• Employ the "Five-Minute Method." You and your spouse should spend five minutes in each room that is bothering you, attacking the largest problems first—make the bed before you put away the blocks, for example. Though you will need to come back to these rooms later, it's amazing how much better you'll feel after each room gets a "lift-me-up!"

18

SPACE MANAGEMENT:
Room Planning and Organization

A child's bedroom starts out with a crib, a dresser, and a changing table. But before you know it, the walls are filled with additional furniture—perhaps a bookcase, another dresser, and eventually a desk. At some point, it becomes obvious that the room doesn't work; there needs to be a new plan. Here's how to improve your child's space through better organization.

CONSIDER THE CHILD

Consider how important this space is to your children. It's where they wake in the morning, dress for the day, play, and study, and where they come for solitude and sleep.

WORTH THE TIME! • Once a year, reevaluate each child's space needs (spring or early summer is a good time). One year you may find that a reading lamp is the only addition you need to make; the next time—perhaps when your son is ready to put away his action figures—you may need to do some serious reorganization. Go to the bedroom and make note of the following elements:

—Is the room shared with a sibling? (A section at the end of the chapter addresses setting up shared space.)

—Is the bedroom a place where your child and friends play?

—What type of games do they play (fantasy play, blocks, dress-ups, board games, etc.)?

—Where does your child change clothes?

—Is the child old enough to get out clothing? Can he open and shut drawers, or is shelving better?

—Can she make the bed?

—If the child is of school age, is homework done in the room? If not, do either of you want this to be the homework room?

—Is your child old enough to have a strong preference as to what hangs on the walls?

Use this information to help guide you as you reorganize.

THE ROOM PLAN

• Create your own room-planning kit using graph and construction paper. Establish a scale (one square = one-half foot is a good size), and measure your child's room, marking the location of all windows and doors. Use construction paper to represent furniture, cutting it to scale.

• As you plan the room, consider:

Function of the various parts of the room. Most bedrooms should accommodate a *dressing area* (near closet and/ or dresser), a *rest area* (the bed and perhaps a comfortable chair), and a *work/play area* (a desk for older kids or open floor space for toddlers).

Traffic flow. Don't place the bed so it blocks access to everything else, for example.

Sunlight. The bright parts of the room are generally best as play or work areas.

ABOUT BEDS

• The bed is probably the most important decision you have to make for a child's room.

A *trundle bed,* where a lower bed pulls out from under the regular bed, offers a convenient arrangement for sleepovers.

A *loft bed,* where a bed space is built five or six feet off the floor (with rails or bars to prevent a fall), provides a way to maximize the use of the room.

A *captain's bed,* with drawers underneath, means additional storage space—particularly appealing to apartment dwellers.

Bunk beds are coveted by most kids and are a logical possibility for families whose youngsters share a room. (Children under age six should not sleep in the top bunk.)

ABOUT FURNITURE

• When you select furniture, choose low-maintenance, durable pieces with smooth edges.

SPACE SAVER!   • Tight on space? Replace a nightstand with a headboard that has storage. You'll need room for a box of tissues, books, and a water glass.

• Open shelving is ideal for younger children because it makes it easier for them to put toys back where they belong.

• Consider a built-in storage unit. Select a unit with several smaller doors rather than one or two large doors, which can be difficult for children to manipulate. Sliding doors are also difficult, so specify doors and drawers that are simple to open and shut.

• Dressers can be bulky, and drawers can be heavy to manipulate, but if you prefer this style, here's my advice:

—Make sure drawers are splinter-free and work easily. Use a silicone spray if the drawers do stick.
—Purchase drawer dividers (available in houseware departments and through catalogs).
—Don't overstuff the drawers. Stack clothing only two or three layers high.

• Most families find that a child-size table and chairs are a good investment—perfect for art projects and tea parties.

• A child's desk should be comfortable for the seven-year-old as well as the teen. (Juvenile desks are outgrown almost immediately.) Select an adult-size desk (nothing huge), and then make certain the chair is suitable for your child's height. As your child grows, you can change chairs.

• Lighting is very important. In addition to an overhead fixture, there should be good supplementary lighting by the bed, by the desk, or in any area that seems dim. A dollhouse shrouded in shadow is much less inviting than one where visibility is good. Also, consider putting the overhead light on a dimmer; you can turn it on low to check a sleeping infant or to dispense medicine to a five-year-old at night.

SMART TIP! • Attaching netting or tack board (painted room color) to the wall provides an attractive, convenient way to display anything from preschool paintings to rock-star posters.

THE ACTUAL REORGANIZING

• Depending on your preference, set aside several blocks of time or one full day to reorganize. Whether or not your child participates depends on his or her age and interest. A toddler should be taken to the playground by a sitter; a school-age child may be just the helper you need.

• Get out a step stool, a spray cleaner, dust cloths, the vacuum, garbage bags, the laundry basket (for those dirty clothes you may find behind the toys!) and about ten medium-to-large boxes, and a marker. Label the biggest boxes: "To Donate," "To Store (Basement)," and "To Put Away Elsewhere in the House." Trash and junk will go in the garbage bags. Now label boxes for the various areas of the room to be created: "Toys," "Arts and Crafts,"

"Games," "Books," "Desk Items," "Bed," and "Dressing Area." (For a child with an advanced interest in a certain hobby, model trains, for example, you would have a specific box to collect all those things as well.)

• You are now going to undertake a basic five-step process for each area of the room:

1. Sift through all belongings and toss or save.
2. Classify by category.
3. Clean area (easier to do as you go along).
4. Arrange area according to new plan.
5. Label.

• For a total redo in a room, clear each area so that you can put things back more efficiently. Working clockwise around the room, start with the items near one wall and sort through each and every one, tossing or saving it and classifying it in an appropriate box.

• Children need to learn to weed out. Don't hesitate to recycle old favorites to younger siblings or cousins, or donate them to a hospital or charity.

• Store items near where they are used. If board games are usually played in the family room, they should be stored there. Likewise, outdoor sports equipment should be stored in the garage, basement, or back hallway.

• Group all items by category or by similar use. Legos should be stored near blocks; costume jewelry should be stored near dress-ups.

• For items you truly can't decide about, try invoking the "Three-Month Rule." Take these items to the basement, garage, or storeroom for three months. If the child misses any item in that time, the treasure is retrievable. If nothing is missed, it can be tossed or donated. (For more information, see Chapter 19.)

ADDITIONAL GUIDELINES

ORGANIZATION PLUS! • Labeling should be age-appropriate. Toddlers can identify the musical-instruments container if it's labeled with an appropriate picture; preschoolers do well with color-coding: Stuffed animals go on the green shelf; etc. Word-and-picture combinations help prereaders with word identification.

• For toddlers, low shelves are terrific for storing toys such as trucks, shape sorters, or a simple dollhouse. If you have more toys than shelving, rotate them. Every two weeks or so, get toys out from the closet to replace the ones on the shelves. The ones that have been out can now be put up high for a time (store in a labeled box). To a toddler, it's as good as going to the toy store!

• Any items requiring supervision, such as Legos, art equipment, or clay, can be stored up high or in a closet to be brought out for special occasions.

• Books should be stored on shelves low enough for your child to reach. Sort through them periodically to weed out any that have been outgrown; put them away for a sibling or donate. Don't give away baby books too quickly. A new reader will delight in having a selection of books he or she can read easily!

• By preschool, children have the capacity to work on a project for awhile and then return to it. Establish a corner of the room where a block city or a doll game can be left out for a day or two.

• Is a messy bed the only thing between your child and a well-organized room? Make your final room investment an attractive (but sturdy) comforter, which can hide a menagerie of animals and a multitude of wrinkles.

WHEN CHILDREN SHARE A ROOM

Children who double up learn cooperation and sharing, and, often, the siblings become especially close friends.

• As children grow older, privacy may become important. Most bedrooms can be divided in some way. A bulletin board, storage cubes, shelving designed as a divider, or a half-wall that permits light but not vision are all possibilities when it comes to creative and practical ways to split the room.

• If you plan to divide the room, move a temporary divider (even a chair or chairs) into the place where you expect the divider to be. This will allow you to check your plan before it's permanent. Try to divide the room so that each child has easy access to the door and so that light comes through to both parts of the room.

• Assign drawers and shelves by height, and be sure that each child has his or her own specific storage space.

• Try to use each child's favorite color somewhere in the room. It can be a wall near their desk or an accessory for the bed.

• Talk with your children about the joys and difficulties of sharing a room. As problems develop, help the kids come up with their own rules.

19

SPACE MANAGEMENT:
Storage Ideas That Work . . .
and Some That Don't

When it comes to storing children's possessions, I hear lots of unusual last-resort solutions: One mother felt the answer was for the family to move, taking little with them; another parent wanted to rent a storage room; yet another trucked things to her in-laws' basement.

There's no need to go to these extremes. Thoughtfully planned space and the right storage systems can hold what most families need. When developing your plan, consider these popular storage aids that work:

STORAGE BASICS

Shelving or a "cubby" system (shelves with dividers), instead of cabinets or drawers, are practical for children's belongings because they make everything visible and accessible. Because it's easy to put something back on a shelf, kids tend to be a little better about putting things away.

WHEN INSTALLING SHELVING

- Make shelves only twelve to fifteen inches deep so items don't become lost at the back of the shelf.
- Shelves should be adjustable.
- Anchor shelves securely to the wall.
- Label everything. If your child cannot yet read, label with a photograph or a sketch, or cut out the picture from the toy's original box.
- Paint the shelves different colors. Teach your children that the crayons and paper go on the yellow shelf, while the games go on the green.
- Add a final coat of polyurethane so that the shelves will be easy to wipe clean.

POPULAR STORAGE AIDS THAT WORK

- ***Baskets.*** A medium-size basket (about twelve to fourteen inches across) can provide a tidy way to keep a few toys in various rooms for your toddler. If he follows you into your bedroom, you'll have something for him to play with while you make the bed. (Rotate these toys from room to room so that your child doesn't get bored with a particular selection.)

Roomy picnic baskets or trunk-size wicker baskets with lids provide wonderful storage for dress-ups. Because there is ample space, clean-up takes less than five minutes.

• *Bins.* These open containers have no lids, meaning that dust can become a problem. Even with that pitfall, I do like bins for blocks and for large, awkward items such as sports equipment.

• *Boxes.* Any sturdy box may be used for storage so long as it's well labeled.

> *Plastic boxes* with lids come in several sizes and are often well worth the investment. They are designed to be stacked and ideal for holding Legos, smaller musical instruments, baseball cards, action figures, toy dishes, dollhouse furniture, small dolls, and doll clothes, etc. Use different colors of boxes (even the transparent ones are sold with lids of different colors) to hold different categories of items (blue for art projects; red for Legos and other construction equipment; green for dolls and accessories).
>
> *School supplies boxes* are just right for crayons, markers, and homework-related items.
>
> *Shoe boxes* can be wonderful homes for paper dolls, craft paraphernalia, parts to a larger toy, or treasures like shells, rocks, or other collectibles.
>
> *Tackle boxes* are sturdy and have strong latches, making them perfect as convenient tool kits for hobbies such as model-building or jewelry-making.
>
> *Cigar boxes* make good keepsake boxes for items such as photos and letters.

• *Car organizer.* This is a fabric "slip cover" that hangs over the back of the front seat and provides shoebag-style organizational space for storage of items ranging from baby toys to older children's puzzle books. These organizers are available through catalogs and at children's supply stores.

• *Cloth mesh bags.* Use these for bath toys (collect the toys and hang the bag over the spout to drain), or to keep together odd-shaped toys with parts such as stacking toys or sorters.

• *Hat (or clothes) rack.* Catalogs and stores now show hat or clothes racks designed as horses, giraffes, and other creative shapes, making them both attractive and handy. Use one in a hallway for coats, or in a child's room for hats, necklaces, or robe and pajamas.

• *Laundry hamper.* Put a hamper wherever your child changes clothes. In the bathroom? In the child's room? (Tuck it in the closet.)

• *Lazy Susans.* Carousel-style lazy Susans are perfect for storing small jars of baby food. Later on, use it to hold items such as glue, tape, and small bottles of paint. Look for other carousel organizers that have special compartments for crayons, markers, paint brushes, and scissors.

• *Zip-lock plastic bags.* These bags are easy to open and close, and make perfect storage pouches for marbles, puzzles, jacks sets, and a myriad of other children's treasures.

POPULAR STORAGE AIDS THAT DON'T WORK

• *Shoe bags.* I'm not a big advocate of using shoe bags for their intended purpose, because the weight of the shoes eventually causes the bag to sag and tear. (Put shoes on a low shelf in the closet.) If you have one that is in good condition, use it to hold art supplies, or suggest to your child that these are "pouches" for storing small stuffed animals.

- *Toy chest.* Don't plan to use a toy box or chest as a catch-all. If small toys are tossed into any type of large container, they never resurface. You can use a toy chest effectively by limiting storage to a single category—dress-ups, balls and sand toys, a large collection of doll clothes, even blankets and linens. (Be certain that the chest has a safety latch that holds the lid open.)

- *Underbed storage.* Only if you're desperate!

FOR BABIES ONLY

- *Baskets (small)* On a changing table, use a small basket to hold rattles for baby to play with during a diaper change.

- *Canisters.* These are perfect for cotton, swabs, hair bows, and anything small that you want to keep handy. Look for plastic or other nonbreakable types with tight-fitting tops so they are difficult for little fingers to open. (As your baby becomes more active, be sure to store dangerous items out of reach.)

- *Cart.* Use a rolling cart to hold a week's worth of diapers. It also comes in handy for storing stuffed animals, toys, or clothing when you're tight on space.

- *Supply caddy.* This is a molded plastic, open-top carry-all (about 8″ × 14″) with a handle, generally sold in hardware stores. A caddy is terrific for diaper-changing and grooming supplies. It's easy to carry if you need to change a diaper elsewhere in the house. One mother bought a second caddy and stocked it with all the items she needed for a nursing session (burp cloth, nursing ointment, extra diaper, portable telephone, and magazine).

• *Toy sheet.* Take any blanket or sheet that you don't mind spreading on the floor and use it as a clean, contained spot for your precrawler and his or her toys. When nap time or evening comes, simply fold it (along with the toys) and tuck it away for the next time.

20

THE TELEPHONE

You probably chuckled the first time your three-year-old answered the phone and then hung up after responding "yes" to what was almost certainly the query, "Is your mommy or daddy there?" Though it is funny, it also illustrates that children aren't born knowing how to handle telephone calls. Whether the calls are incoming or outgoing, there *is* a manageable, efficient way to teach your children how to use the telephone.

SETTING UP A TELEPHONE CENTER

• Keep the following by each telephone:

—Pencil or pen (if yours tend to disappear, buy one of the pens on a cord to fasten onto the telephone).
—Pad of paper.

• Near your most frequently used phones, have:

—List of emergency numbers.
—Local or area telephone book.
—Children's personalized telephone book (described later).

• On each telephone, tape a label with your last name, house address, and the telephone number written on it. (If an emergency occurs, you want to make it easy for anyone using the telephone to get help.)

HOW TO CREATE A CHILDREN'S TELEPHONE BOOK

WORTH THE TIME! Our children's social—and phoning—circles are generally quite large. To manage all the phone numbers of your children's class and teammates, you'll need to do some organizing.

1. Buy:

—Thin looseleaf binder, 9½″ × 12″. Label it "Children's Telephone Book."
—Colored dividers. Label one for each child.
—Gummed reinforcement circles.

2. Collect:

—The class lists of each of your children (include lists from years past if you still refer to them).

    Label each with child's name, grade, and the year.

—Add to this collection any telephone lists of your children's extracurricular groups (Brownies, soccer team), and label.

—On a separate sheet of paper list other telephone numbers that should be included (neighbors, relatives, etc.).

3. Assemble:

—Sort chronologically using the dividers to separate each child's lists. Put the most recent lists on top, and place them all in the binder.

Show your children the system you've established, and place the book near your most frequently used telephone.

TEACHING YOUR CHILDREN TELEPHONE ETIQUETTE

• Preschoolers should be shown how to hold the receiver properly and speak directly into it.

• Teach your children *not* to identify themselves to unknown callers.

• Once the caller has indicated to whom he wishes to speak, your child should refrain from bellowing, "Daddy!" The caller should be asked politely to wait a moment, and Daddy should be told at close range that he has a telephone call.

• If you can't take the call, teach your child to say, "My mother can't come to the phone right now." A school-age child can offer to take a message; a preschooler should suggest the person call back.

• When your child is six or older, teach her about the other buttons—"hold," "call-waiting," and "redial."

• Rehearse a few telephone calls with your children so that they will understand what is expected of them.

• Older children should learn how to use an answering machine . . . and how to save calls while resetting it.

MESSAGE-TAKING

IMPORTANT! • If your children are being given the responsibility of taking messages, then they should learn to take *complete* messages. Here's what to teach:

—Get caller's first and *last* names.
—Ask for telephone number.
—Write legibly.
—At the end of the call, read the message back to the caller (including the name and telephone number) so that he or she has an opportunity to make corrections.

• Create a form (see below) and photocopy it; leave a supply by each telephone.

Message for _____ Date: _____

Caller's Name: _____ _____

Telephone Number:
　/ / will call again　　/ / please call back

　Message:

• Leave all family messages in a predesignated spot.

IN CASE OF EMERGENCY

• By the time your child is two, begin teaching her to say her full name, address, and telephone number. By age three, most children can repeat this information clearly.

• If you have 911 as your emergency number, start teaching children over two to dial it.

• If your community does not have 911, some experts recommend using fingernail polish to put a red dot by the "0."

• If you have one of the newer phones that can be programmed to automatically dial certain numbers, then set yours up with access to emergency personnel. Stickers (fire hat, red cross for ambulance, badge for policeman) can be purchased and affixed to the appropriate automatic-dial button. (If your child suspects fire, he or she should be instructed to go next door before calling for help.)

• Stress to your child that emergencies are rare, but that it is important to know how to handle them. Talk about some possible scenarios. You might ask: "What if the babysitter fell?" Or: "What if your little sister got cut badly, and I sent you in to call for help?" Rehearse with your children what they might say. Teach them not to hang up after an emergency call. The call can be traced if the phone remains off the hook.

WHEN YOU'RE ON THE PHONE

To children, the telephone brings in an unseen foe; the accessible parent is now unavailable! No wonder children are so demanding when we're on the phone. Here's what helps:

- Rules depend on the child's age, but, in general, ask children not to interrupt you.

- A cordless telephone lets you continue to talk and supervise the kids at the same time. Since their activities can continue, they'll usually complain less.

- With younger children, plan to make your calls during a favorite television program, put on a videotape, or offer to supervise water play in the kitchen sink while you talk.

- Be specific about the fact that you have some phoning to do, and estimate the length of time you'll be on the phone: "I'll be finished when your program is over," for example.

SMART TIP! • To be prepared for incoming calls, stow some special activities (stickers, activity books, etc.) near the phone so that you can offer a positive distraction.

- Try putting a restless toddler on your lap during a call. Often they'll calm down by being physically close to you. (Offering juice or a cracker doesn't hurt either!)

- Sometimes you simply have to get off the phone and delay your calls. Perhaps five minutes resettling a toddler or a stern conversation with a ten-year-old will be enough to let you finish the phoning you need to do.

Organize Your Family!

If you have questions about organization, or additional suggestions you would like to share, please write to Ronni Eisenberg & Associates, c/o Kate Kelly, 11 Rockwood Drive, Larchmont, NY 10538.

About the Authors

Ronni Eisenberg, author of *Organize Yourself!*, has given a multitude of workshops, lectures, and demonstrations across the country on how to get organized. She lives and works in New York City with her husband and three children. Kate Kelly is a professional writer who owns and operates her own publishing business. She lives in Westchester County, New York, with her husband and three children.